JANUSZ KORCZAK

GHETTO DIARY

WITH AN INTRODUCTION
BY BETTY JEAN LIFTON

Yale University Press
New Haven and London

First published in 1978 by Holocaust Library
This edition published in the United States by Yale University
Press 2003

Printed in the United States of America.

ISBN 978-0-300-09742-9
ISBN 0-300-09742-5 (pbk. : alk. paper)

Library of Congress Control Number: 2002115529

A catalogue record for this book is available from the British
Library.

The paper in this book meets the guidelines for permanence and
durability of the Committee on Production Guidelines for Book
Longevity of the Council on Library Resources.

10   9   8   7

CONTENTS

WHO WAS JANUSZ KORCZAK?
by Betty Jean Lifton   vii

GHETTO DIARY
by Janusz Korczak

Part One   3

Part Two   79

Korczak with his children

WHO WAS JANUSZ KORCZAK?

Betty Jean Lifton

Janusz Korczak, a renowned Polish Jewish writer and pediatrician and one of the world's first children's rights advocates, often said that life is a strange dream. But his death proved even stranger. Today he is remembered not for the way he lived, but for the way he died.

Korczak became a legend in Europe when he refused offers to save his own life and chose to march with the orphans under his care in a dignified procession through the streets of the Warsaw ghetto to the trains that were to carry them to "Resettlement in the East" but took them instead to the death camp Treblinka. The Poles claim Korczak as a martyr, who would have been canonized if he had converted; the Israelis claim him as one of the Thirty-Six Just Men, whose pure souls make possible the world's salvation. UNESCO declared 1978–79 the Year of Janusz Korczak, to coincide with the Year of the Child and the centenary of his birth.

During the last three months of his life, Korczak was working on a manuscript that has become known as the Ghetto Diary. He began it as a personal memoir, shortly after Warsaw fell to the Germans in 1939, and about a year before the ghetto was established. As Nazi troops patrolled the streets outside his famed Jewish orphanage on 92 Krochmalna Street, he wrote the first line: "Reminiscences make a sad, depressing literature." Depressing because everyone starts out with ambitious plans only to learn with old age that life did not turn out as they expected.

Certainly he did not expect at the age of sixty-one to be writing a memoir in occupied Warsaw—in what he called "the hour of reckoning in the saddest hospital in the world." But he did sense that this was a perilous time, and time was running out. Korczak likened working on his project to digging a well. "A firm grip on the shovel. Let's go. One, two; one, two." He will uncover "subterranean springs" and "browse through memories," back to the era when Imperial Russia occupied his part of partitioned Poland. Searching for style, even as he searches for himself, he sets one scene as a dialogue between two "old codgers" warming themselves in the sun while ruminating on why they are still alive. The first one has lived a conventional life of moderation. In contrast, our author recalls landing in the "cooler" with other young Polish intellectuals while resisting the Czar's secret police; being conscripted as a doctor during the Russo-Japanese War and World War I; and staking his life on "a single card"—the care of destitute children. He's a veteran not only of war, but of life. Now, though his body is "falling to pieces—adhesions, aches, ruptures, scars"—he can "still kick pretty hard."

When asked if he has children and grandchildren, he boasts: "Two hundred."

"You like to joke don't you?" exclaims the first old codger.

Korczak did like to joke—he had a wry, ironic, self-deprecating humor. But as the Germans tightened their noose around the city over the next year and forced him to move his Jewish orphanage into the Warsaw ghetto, it was no joking matter. He stopped writing for two and a half years. During that time all his energies were taken up with finding provisions for his orphans and young staff. He defied the Germans by wearing his Polish uniform and refusing to put on the mandated white armband with the blue Star of David. He felt it demeaned the Jewish star to be used in such a way, but this resistance almost cost him his life. When he protested to the Gestapo that his orphanage's potatoes had been confiscated during its move to the ghetto, he was thrown into the notorious Pawiak prison for not wearing his armband. He survived only because one of his former orphans had the contacts and funds to get him out.

Korczak had been in the ghetto for a year and a half when he returned to the diary in May 1942 and continued dredging his personal well. "One, two; one two." We can surmise that he started writing again because of the increasing violence of Nazi death squads, beginning with Bloody Friday, two weeks before, when members of the underground press were summarily executed. Also the alarming rumors of impending mass deportations to unknown destinations had now become impossible to ignore and told him that he should not delay any longer.

Still the resister, Korczak avoids mentioning the sinister world outside as he sets the scene at 5 AM in his ghetto orphanage, which is located in a former businessman's club. "The month of May is cold this year," he writes, as if there has been no interruption. He sleeps in the west wing, the infirmary, and Stepha Wilczynska, his loyal colleague, who has worked with him for the past thirty years, is in the east wing, with the girls. His bed is in the middle of the room, where "for inspiration" he keeps the scarce bottle of vodka (which later will be replaced with five glasses of raw alcohol mixed with hot water) next to his bed, along with black bread and a jug of water. He writes with a pen or pencil, sharpened on both ends by Felek, a former orphan now on staff, who types the pages each morning. Felek is the son of Azrylewewicz, the ailing old tailor, who also has a bed in the infirmary and keeps Korczak awake with his moaning.

By now Korczak's body had fallen to pieces, but he was still kicking pretty hard as, every midnight or dawn, he forced his hand to record his fragmented thoughts. His notations were often no more than a terse shorthand that he hoped to fill in later. The diary flashes back to scenes of his own childhood as he free-associates from some interaction with the orphans, who take over many pages with their coughs, their own diaries, their yearning for trees and flowers. He was living in the future, too, with lists of his literary projections and fantasies of a peaceful world, where the only war would be of poets and musicians in Olympic games, or a war for the most beautiful prayer in a world hymn to God once a year. At one point, he adds slyly: "I have forgotten to mention that now, too, a war is going on." But this "district of the damned"—where half a million people were squeezed in on top of one another without sufficient food, housing, or heat, and where typhus had decimated those who had not already succumbed to malnutrition and cold—gave his writing an urgency that escalated along with the increase in Nazi violence and cruelty.

Clearly, this is not a ghetto diary like that of Emanuel Ringleblum or Chaim Kaplan, who took on a historic responsibility to record everything they observed in the Warsaw ghetto. Korczak's diary reveals how a spiritual and moral man struggled to shield innocent children from the atrocities of the adult world during one of history's darkest times. Writing is the only weapon any writer has when he or she is trapped and there is no place to go but inward. If such a diary had been written by Chekhov, Doestoevsky, or Gorky under similar circumstances, the reader would already be familiar with the author's life, his work, and his circle of friends. But just as

Korczak asks in the diary, "Ever heard of Nalkowski? The world knows nothing of many great Poles," we might ask how many in the English-speaking world have heard of Korczak or read his books for both adults and children, most of them still untranslated from the Polish?

Who was Janusz Korczak? Born Henryk Goldzmit in Warsaw in 1878 or 1879 (his father delayed registering his birth) into an assimilated family, he was already famous as Janusz Korczak (his pen name) for his autobiographical novels at the turn of the century and as an educator who gave up his medical practice to set up the first progressive orphanages in Warsaw for destitute children. He founded the first children's newspaper, *The Little Review,* and had a radio program as the Old Doctor, whose warmth and wit were much in the style of Will Rogers. His play, *Senate of Madmen,* starring one of Poland's leading actors, foreshadowed the rise of fascism in Poland in the thirties. As an educator, he wrote books for parents and teachers with titles like *How to Love a Child* (written on the battlefields of World War I) and *The Child's Right to Respect.* His children's book *King Matt the First,* as beloved as *Peter Pan,* is about a child king who yearns to make reforms that will improve the lives of children. Matt tries valiantly, only to have his kingdom taken over by three neighboring countries, much as Poland had been partitioned the century before by Russia, Austria, and Prussia.

Korczak may have been a visionary and a dreamer, but he was also a pragmatist who had no illusions about human nature. "Reformers come to a bad end," an old doctor (much like himself) tells King Matt. "Only after their death do people see that they were right and erect monuments in their honor." Korczak has no grave, but there is a monument to him in the Jewish cemetery in Warsaw and in many countries, as well as streets and schools that

bear his name. It would not have been lost on him, however, that everywhere in the world, children, whom he
called the future of civilization, are still suffering from
poverty, disease, and malnutrition, and as victims of war.

In his life and work, Korczak emerges as a cross between the magical Dr. Doolittle and the pediatrician
Benjamin Spock, the healer Anton Chekhov and the re-
former Leo Tolstoy. He is often compared to other inno-
vative European educators like Johann Pestalozzi, who
set up republics for destitute children, but he also had
the psychological sensibility of Erik Erikson in his understanding of the meaning and seriousness of play.

The incredible accomplishment of this memoir is that
Korczak—his body emaciated, his heart failing—had the
discipline and will to keep digging his well after trudging
all day on his swollen legs to collect money and provisions to keep his orphans alive. The diary has flashes of
Korczak's droll wit, ironic humor, and philosophic mus-
ings, but written under such desperate conditions, it is
not vintage Korczak. He gradually lost control of his nar-
rative, his temper, and his concentration. At one point,
he paused to ask why he was digressing, what was it he
was trying to say? Rereading his manuscript after two
months, he was in despair: "I could hardly understand
it." He wonders if it is possible to understand someone
else's reminiscences, let alone his own. His very identity
seems at stake in this segregated Jewish quarter as he
wonders if it is any longer possible to be both a Pole and a
Jew (which he considered himself until the Nazis declared otherwise), as he careens between his faith in the
goodness of people and his confrontation with pure evil.
In the loneliness that was his only constant now, as it had
been throughout his life, this despairing Jewish savior of
children, who lived in a Catholic country, yearned for a
confidant, a confessor, an understanding ear to hear his

"lament." The diary and its future readers must serve this purpose.

Those who want to learn about Korczak's background will find shards of information strewn about in the manuscript. The scenes from his childhood were like nuggets of gold for me when I was writing his biography. The diary clears up the widespread confusion about whether Korczak was Jewish because his name is Polish and his books were written in Polish, not Yiddish. He tells us of his own shock on learning as a five-year-old that he was a Jew from the Polish janitor's son, who threatened him with a dark place much like Hell if he did not do his bidding. We do not know if his father, Jozef, a lawyer, took him to synagogue or had him bar mitzvahed, but he passed on to him the aspirations of his own father, a physician, to liberate the Jews from their segregated lives and propel them into Polish culture. Jozef supported craft schools conducted in Polish for Jewish children to enable them to enter the mainstream workforce. To help the Poles understand Jewish history and customs, he wrote a book on Talmudic divorce law in Polish, and a series of minibiographies of Jews and Poles of "high moral spirit." The goal of Korczak's father and grandfather was to build a strong bridge between the Poles and Jews.

"I ought to say a good deal about my father: I pursue in life that which he strove for and for which my grandfather tortured himself for many years," Korczak writes in the diary. Embedded in that sentence are both the dream and the pain of assimilated Jews. Korczak was striving to reinforce that bridge when he made Polish the language in his Jewish orphanage; co-directed a second orphanage in Warsaw for poor Catholic children; and wrote hilarious books that have become classics about his experiences as a counselor in both Jewish and Polish summer camps: *Moski, Joski and Srule* and *Jozki, Jaszki and Franki*. He learned at camp that all children are alike because they speak the common language of childhood. They laugh at the same things and when they feel the weight of life, they weep at the same things.

Korczak's father, like the ghost of Hamlet's father, haunts the first part of the diary. "I am the son of a madman," he writes of this accomplished father, who died at the age of fifty-two after years of hospitalization when Korczak was eighteen. There has been speculation that Jozef may have had syphilis, and that Korczak never married for fear of inheriting his mental illness. He felt deserted by this dead father. "Every madman is just a pretender who couldn't cope and took the easy way out," a character declares in his play *Senate of Madmen*. This early trauma also reveals itself in an unpublished novel called *Suicide*, but his father's erratic behavior made him determined never to lose control or desert those dependent on him. Insanity in the individual and in the world became themes in his work and would run through the ghetto diary as the madness of that world closed in on him.

Children became Korczak's savior in his youth, just as he would become theirs. He forgot his own anxieties while tutoring pampered, rich boys, much like he had been, in order to help support his mother, and in the process developed some of the creative strategies that he would later use in his orphanages. He lived with his overly protective mother well into adulthood, but some of his tenderest and most alarming memories of childhood revolve around that charming, lost father, "that not particularly reliable pedagogue," who was capable of flying into rages and calling him a "gawk or a clod." Despite his mother's objections, his father took him and his older sister, Anka, on excursions to Nativity plays and bought them soda ice with pineapple juice, which made the boy ill.

At Christmastime, it was Korczak's father who invited in the unemployed construction workers who went from house to house performing a puppet play—a performance that is "beautiful, and scary." The scariest part came after it was over, for then an old man with a sack appeared to take up donations. The boy, "trembling with excitement," would toss his little coins into the sack. The old man would peer inside, shake his long white beard, and say: "Very little, very little, young gentleman, a bit more."

There, in the ghetto, Korczak remembers that "it was an instructive hour" because the old man was "insatiable" and his sack was "bottomless." The old man with the sack had taught Korczak a great deal: "The hopelessness of defense against persistent requests and unbounded demands that are impossible to meet. At first, you give eagerly, then less enthusiastically, from a sense of duty, then, following the laws of inertia, from habit and without heart, and then resentfully, angrily, with despair." By the time he was writing this, the perversity of fate had turned Korczak into the old man with the sack. Each morning in the ghetto he got up, slung a sack over his aching shoulder, and went out to makes his rounds of wealthy contacts and social service agencies to plead, then demand, money and food for his two hundred children. He was as relentless as the old man: no matter what they gave, it was never enough. People began to dread his calls. In the diary, Korczak rants about those who have gone beyond inertia and despair to downright refusal to contribute any more to the "Orphans' Aid" fund.

Some of the people who tried to keep giving, despite their diminished circumstances, were the philanthropists who had supported Korczak's Krochmalna Street orphanage, which opened in 1912 with a hundred Jewish boys and girls, ages seven to fourteen. Members of Warsaw society had been amazed that the famous Janusz Korczak would give up his literary career and successful medical practice to take care of dirty, runny-nosed kids. They did not understand that medicine was no longer enough for this visionary pediatrician. "The road I have chosen toward my goal is neither the shortest nor the most convenient," he told an interviewer. "But it is the best for me—because it is my own. I found it not without effort or pain." Part of the difficulty in making the decision lay in assuring himself that he was not betraying medicine. He reasoned that medicine is involved only with curing the sick child, but he had a chance to cure the whole child. As a scientist he could use the orphanage as a laboratory for clinical observation; as an educator, he could be the "sculptor of the child's soul."

The children's republic was designed as a just community where its young citizens would have their own parliament, newspaper, and court of peers. They would learn consideration and fair play and develop responsibility for others that they would carry into the adult world. Korczak was a pioneer in what we now call "moral education." He was concerned not with teaching children their ABCs—they went to public school for that— but with the grammar of ethics. At the same time, he wanted to teach adults how to understand children and treat them fairly. His Declaration of Children's Rights stated that children have a right to be loved, respected, and given optimal conditions in which to grow. They have a right to be taken seriously. They are not people of tomorrow, but of today. They should be allowed to become whomever they are meant to be: "The unknown person inside each child is the hope for the future."

But Korczak knew that children of deprivation are vulnerable and need help to overcome vices that can defeat them. As a form of tonic, Pan Doctor, as the orphans called him, devised ingenious strategies—his "pedagogical arsenal"—to help his charges strengthen their will. One favorite was the make-believe gambling casino he set up for them to bet on how many fights they would have each week, until they were motivated to have none. However, he considered the children's court of peers the cornerstone of his system, because it would show the children that there could be justice even in an unjust world. Rather than poking someone in the nose because he hurt you, a child could call out "I sue you," and sign his or her name on the list of court cases that were heard each Saturday morning. Five children with no cases against them that week were the judges, who followed a Code of Laws that Korczak had drawn up. The first hundred articles were based on forgiveness. Only in the most serious circumstances would a child be charged with one hundred or more. "The court is not justice, but it should strive for justice," Korczak wrote in the Preamble to the Code. "The court is not truth, but it should strive for truth. Judges may make mistakes. They may punish for acts they themselves are guilty of. But it is shameful if a judge consciously hands down an unjust verdict."

Behind Korczak's creative techniques was a keen psychological understanding of children that came from years of practice, experience that most doctors, including Sigmund Freud, who worked with adults, did not have. "I am a doctor by training, a pedagogue by chance, a writer by passion, and a psychologist by necessity," he once told a friend. He could have added that while the psychologist helped the children win the battle with themselves in ways that would not undermine their pride, the doctor took notes on his clinical observations of their height and weight, and sleeping habits, which he hoped to compile in a "thick volume."

As part of his resistance to the Nazis, Korczak kept the

same structure and routine in his ghetto orphanage that existed in his pre-war children's republic. Every Saturday morning, the children were weighed, the court of peers met and handed down its verdicts, and he read aloud the orphanage newspaper. He added an underground school in the orphanage, which included Hebrew in the curriculum to prepare those children who might want to go to Palestine in the future.

Korczak was not a Zionist, but he had taken short trips to Palestine in 1934 and 1936 when anti-Semitism was on the rise in Poland. Staying in Kibbutz Ein Harod at the invitation of some of his former students, he marveled at Jews working the land. "Jewish brains are resting," he quipped. However, he resisted invitations to settle there permanently. "I'm old," he said. "My teeth are falling out, also the hair on my head. This Hebrew of yours needs young and strong teeth which can crush every nut." When he returned from Palestine in 1936, Korczak was attacked in the right wing press for going there. During those "wicked, shameful, destructive, prewar years," he resigned as co-director of the Polish orphanage after the board asked him if he was a Zionist. He was no longer allowed to represent delinquent children in court, and he lost his radio show as the Old Doctor, despite a letter written in his defense by one of the Polish staff: "Korczak was the greatest humanist on the air in Poland. He spoke to children as if they were adults and to adults as if they were children."

As fascism continued to spread in Poland, Korczak kept putting off a return to Palestine. It was not only because he could not leave the children in such dire times, but he could not leave Warsaw, his beloved city. "Warsaw is mine and I am hers," he writes in the diary. "I'll say no more. I am hers. Together with her I have rejoiced and I have grieved. Her weather was my weather, her rain, her soil, mine as well. We grew up together. Warsaw has been my workshop. Here are my landmarks and my graves."

In late 1938, however, when Warsaw seemed no longer Warsaw, he made plans to visit Palestine for four months in October 1939. He asked a friend to find a modest room in Jerusalem where he could put his Polish bible on a small table and write a children's bible—which would include the childhoods of King David and Jesus. Explaining his delay, he wrote: "A man is responsible to his own spirit, his own mode of thought—that is his workshop. I ask myself: Is it too late? No. Had I gone earlier, I would have felt like a deserter. One has to remain at one's post until the very last moment." By then it was the last moment. On September 1, the Germans invaded Poland.

Korczak's thoughts turned repeatedly to the future and to Palestine in the diary. He rejects the idea that he might participate in building a new order in Poland because (his droll humor still intact, even if his body was not) it would mean having a nine to five job. Instead, he imagines that he will create a huge orphanage in northern Galilee. He will live in one room on the terrace of a flat roof with transparent walls, so he will not miss a single sunrise or sunset, and so that writing at night he might be able to look now and again at the stars. He will visit Warsaw every year for a few weeks to talk over "important, eternal problems."

Meanwhile, in the ghetto, time, like everything else, had run amok, the past intruding into the present. The only public transportation now was horse-drawn trams. Carriages and automobiles had been replaced by pedicabs—bicycles with small seats attached for passengers. At first, Korczak avoided them, but as it became more difficult for him to get around on his aching legs, he began to rationalize that taking them would help the pedicab men make a living. Unlike the "quarrelsome, noisy

and spiteful" droshsky drivers of prewar days, the pedicab men were "gentle and quiet, like horses or oxen."

Korczak struggled to keep his spirits up, but this educator, who could not bear to see a child suffer from in-
justice or an unkind word, who had taken a vow to uphold
the cause of children and to defend their rights, had to
pass dead or dying children on the street every day. He
records without comment that three boys playing horse
and driver on the sidewalk were annoyed that the body of
a dead child was in their way. He does not tell us that
he tried unsuccessfully to get the Judenrat (the Jewish
Council) to provide a special place where terminally ill
children, comforted by laypeople, could die with dignity.

Instead, Korczak describes his difficulties trying to
save the orphans at a public shelter ("a slaughterhouse
and morgue") for one thousand children at 39 Dznielna
Street. He rails against the corrupt staff, which had been
siphoning off provisions there while the children were lying in filth and dying untended at the rate of ten to twelve
a day. Despite his efforts, the mortality rate remained at
sixty percent. When one of the devoted nurses, Miss Wittlin, died of tuberculosis, he writes: "The salt of the earth
dissolves—the manure remains."

More than once "during the dark hours," Korczak, the
doctor, pondered the killing (putting to sleep) of infants
and old people in the ghetto. Suicide and euthanasia are
subjects to which he keeps returning. Like his close
friend, Adam Czerniakow, Chairman of the Judenrat,
Korczak kept pills in his possession so that suicide could
be an option. The pills gave him a feeling of control over
his fate, so that he could choose "freely" when to exit, but
they also reminded him of his suicidal thoughts after his
mother's death, for which he still felt responsible. While
evaluating possible typhoid carriers during the Russo-
Polish war of 1919–1920, he neglected to wash his hands

and became infected. His mother caught typhoid and died while caring for him. Korczak tells us that he was saved from doing away with himself not only by his sister's refusal to join him in a suicide pact, but also by the psychic force of "some new daydream" that he might develop into a short story. He invented a machine that could purge the world of inhuman people; he found the magic word and became the ruler of light. He called these daydreams "Oddities" or "Strange Happenings." Now when he wakens at night in a sweat from nightmares—without an armband after curfew, on a train where there are bodies of dead children—he turns those daydreams or creates new ones for the power to defeat evil.

For the first two weeks in July, when smugglers (a main source of food and supplies) were being slaughtered along the walls, on the streets, in the courtyards, Korczak, the writer, escapes by soaring over the ghetto walls to a planet called Ro. The astronomer who lives on it, Professor Zi, can convert heat radiation into moral power on his "astropsychomicrometer." He can bestow order and tranquility everywhere except on "that restless spark, Planet Earth." Brooding on the wars and smoldering battlefields down there, Professor Zi wonders if he should simply put an end to this senseless, bloody game. But with the compassion of the Old Doctor, he concludes: "Planet Earth is still young. And a beginning is painful labor."

Professor Zi was in control up there on Planet Ro, but Janusz Korczak has no control down here in the smoldering ghetto, except in his children's republic. Still the inventive pedagogue, he makes a game out of catching the flies that swarm over the toilet buckets. The children who catch fifteen flies can have a first-class toilet seat over their bucket. Those with only ten flies have a second-class

"bucket-stool-with-a-hole combination." He is thrilled
when one of the boys asks: "May I pay the flies later? I
can't wait," and another offers to catch his flies for him.
"Community good will—what a mighty force," Korczak
writes. His children are still generous to one another.
There is hope for the world.

Yet, his newest daydreams reflect the hopelessness
taking over the ghetto. There is a sardonic edge to one
called "Euthanasia," in which people can apply for death
when life has lost its meaning. Endless details had to be
considered: the application, medical examination, consultation with a psychologist, perhaps a confession, perhaps psychoanalysis, and the location and method of
death. Over the next two weeks as the Nazi violence escalated along with more rumors of deportations in other
cities, Korczak returns to his "Euthanasia" scenario,
where one could at least be in control of one's own death.
He wants to die "consciously," in possession of his faculties, unlike his mad father.

By now, the children were mooning about "like old
people in a sanitarium," comparing symptoms. He
sensed their "weariness, discouragement, anger, mutiny,
mistrust, resentment, and longing." The seriousness of
their diaries hurt, making him realize that he needed to
think of something to help them transcend their present
suffering. During the past year, he had held High Holi-
day services in the orphanage, celebrated Hannukah and
Purim, and organized a Passover seder, just as he had in
pre-war days, because he believed prayer was important
for the orphans. He had also arranged for talented musicians and street singers to come in and teach them Yiddish and Hebrew songs, and for professional people to
talk about their former work. Now he decided the children might enjoy becoming the performers. His interest
in Eastern philosophy led him to choose the play *The*

Post Office, written by the Indian writer and philosopher Rabindranath Tagore, whose empathy for children was much like his own. The production, which took place on July 18—four days before deportations were announced and three weeks before the young actors would march to their deaths—has also become legendary. In the play, Amal, a gentle and imaginative orphan adopted by a poor couple, is confined to his room with a serious illness, shut in from the outside world, like everyone in the ghetto, awaiting an uncertain future. He longs to fly to that land to which the King's doctor, greater than the one he has now, will lead him by the hand. The invited guests gasp along with Amal when the royal doctor suddenly appears and orders all the doors and windows to be opened. Amal's pain is gone, and he can see the stars twinkling on the other side of the darkness.

Asked why he chose that play, Korczak is reported to have said that he wanted to help the children face death without fear. But in his diary, he makes only a short notation about the afternoon: "Applause, handshakes, smiles, efforts at cordial conversation." The children seemed so natural in their parts, he wonders what would happen if they could continue in their roles the next day. He decides that illusions would be a good topic for his Wednesday talk with the orphanage staff, then sets off for grim reality—the Dzielna Street orphanage.

Rumors, impossible to verify, continued to spread through the ghetto that Jews were being gassed in other cities and that railroad cars were waiting to deport everyone from the Warsaw ghetto. Korczak's Polish disciples on the Aryan side also heard the rumors, and sent Igor Newerly, his former secretary, into the ghetto disguised as a water and sewer inspector with a false identity card to bring Korczak out. According to Newerly, Korczak refused to abandon the children at such a perilous time.

He did, however, promise to send Newerly the diary he was working on for safekeeping.

July 22 was Korczak's sixty-fourth birthday. It was also the day the Gestapo informed Czerniakow that the deportations, which they had assured him would not happen, were to begin immediately. By 4 PM that afternoon, six thousand people were to be at the Umschlagplatz, a large loading area just north of the ghetto, where freight trains were waiting to take them to "Resettlement in the East." The only exemptions would be members of the Judenrat and their families and essential service units, such as hospital and factory workers. Korczak surely stood in the hysterical crowds looking at the notices posted on the ghetto walls, but rather than accept his inability to alter the surreal events of that day, he did battle where he could. In the diary, he rails against the order that fifty children from a hospital close to the Umschlagplatz are to be evacuated to the Dzielna Street orphanage. And he notes that the old tailor, Azryl, has died. "Oh, how hard it is to live, how easy to die!"

Five days passed before Korczak reports on "a marvellous big moon" overhead and laments that he cannot calm this "unfortunate, insane quarter," as if the whole ghetto had become his orphanage, and he was responsible for everyone in it. As with other sinister events, he does not describe the turmoil as the first deportees—prisoners, inhabitants of refugee centers, and street beggars—were rounded up and taken off in horse-drawn carts that would become known as death wagons. Nor does he tell us that he has been busy trying to set up a factory in the orphanage so that his children would be considered too essential to be moved. He is not a reporter, after all, he is still an educator, a moral philosopher, whose energies must be conserved to save children and to dig his well, before it goes dry. What is happening in the ghetto—"A Prison. A plague-stricken area. A mating ground. A lunatic asylum. A casino. Monaco. The stake—your head"—is beyond his "Strange Happenings." He has lost touch with Professor Zi on Planet Ro. "It has been a long time since I blessed the world," he writes. "I tried to tonight. It didn't work."

The freight cars had been operating for five chaotic days, with people being dragged from their homes or seized on the streets to fill the transport quotas, when, with scathing irony, Korczak makes what would be his only mention of Resettlement in the diary. It is a long monologue called "History's Program," delivered by an SS officer (in less horrific times, he could have been played by Charlie Chaplin), who brags about the "gigantic enterprise" the Germans are running. "Its name is war. We work in a planned, disciplined manner, methodically. Your petty interests, ambitions, sentiments, whims, claims, resentments do not concern us. . . . Jews go East. No bargaining . . . you must take the risk. You must listen my friend, to History's program speech about the new chapter."

Korczak did not want to listen. He had his own program. He countered the words he had given the SS man on why the Gestapo must clear the ghetto with his own defiant response: WHY DO I CLEAR THE TABLE? After a touch of his old wry humor, that it could be because he likes to pretend to be diligent, or to fend off someone coming to see him on "important" business, he gives the real reason. He collects the dishes himself to see the cracked plates, the bent spoons, the scratches on the bowls, and to show the children that "there should be no clean or dirty work, no purely physical or mental workers." This had always been his philosophy. More than once he infuriated the staff at the Dzielna Street orphanage by shaking hands with the charwoman; before the war he liked to shock pompous professors by saying that "Old nannies and construction workers are often better pedagogues than a doctor of psychology." Clearing the table, then, was an act of resistance to prove that he would not abandon his rituals and sense of order, which were the only ballast he had to hold his little republic firmly to its mooring.

Every day brought so many "strange and sinister experiences and sensations" that Korczak has completely ceased to dream. He did not tell us that Czerniakow committed suicide with the pills he kept in his office drawer rather than sign the Gestapo order of deportation. But on Saturday morning, August 1, Korczak admitted that he did not want to get out of bed. For the first time he was not interested in the children's weight, the court decisions, or reading the orphanage newspaper aloud. He willed his depleted body to get up and go through the routine, but he noticed that while the new children might listen carefully to the orphanage newspaper, the old timers knew that they would not learn that which was important to them. And he knew that he could not tell them, because he also did not know how to make sense of the grotesque things that were going on outside. The desperate life in the ghetto now breaks through his resistance and takes over the diary. "What matters is that all of this did happen," he writes. "The destitute beggars suspended between prison and hospital. The slave work. Debased faith, family, motherhood. The marketing of all spiritual commodities."

A few days before the end, Korczak was frantic that Esterka, the apprentice teacher who had directed *The Post Office,* was seized on the street in one of the Aktions. His powerlessness to save her threw him into the hopeless depression he had been fighting off until then. His world was so radically altered, he had no more coping skills. And his children were hungry. After his mother's death, he wrote a prayer book, *Alone With God,* in which eighteen people, among them a new mother, a child, an artist, all bargain with God to have their wishes granted. Now he was ready to bargain as he "carved" a prayer out of hunger and misery: "Our father who art in heaven. Our daily bread. Bread."

In the final entry of August 5 or August 6 (it is not clear in the diary), Korczak is watering the "poor orphanage plants," which had been smuggled into the ghetto by his Polish friends. He muses about the young German soldier standing with his rifle by the ghetto wall across the street. The soldier was not shooting at him, even though his "bald head in the window" would make a "splendid target." Korczak tries to see him as a young man with an identity other than a killer with a gun. "Perhaps he was a village teacher, a street sweeper in Liepzig, a waiter in Cologne." He considers waving his hand in a friendly gesture. He writes what will be the final words of his ghetto diary: "Perhaps he doesn't even know that things are as they are? He may have arrived only yesterday from far away . . ."

It was Korczak who did not know what things were. Early that morning the area around the Small Ghetto, where the orphanage was situated, had been cordoned off by SS men, Ukrainian and Latvian troops. He and the children were sitting down to their meager breakfast when they heard the dread call: "All Jews out."

We can be certain that Korczak tried to reassure the children as they lined up fearfully, clutching their little flasks of water, their few possessions, their diaries. He might have told them that they were on their way to their summer camp, but he did not believe in lying to children. Perhaps he told them they were going on a train trip somewhere to the East, and that he would be there to keep them safe. Korczak may have held onto a small hope that this was true, but even a man of his vivid fantasy could not have imagined what lay in wait for him and the children. No one had yet escaped from Treblinka to reveal the truth: they were not going East, but sixty miles northeast of Warsaw to immediate extermination in gas chambers. Treblinka was not even an overnight stay.

We know from survivors who watched from behind closed shutters, and from Gestapo records, that Korczak, hatless, in high military boots, holding two young children by the hand, was at the head of the orderly procession of 192 children and 10 staff members, including the loyal Stefa, who had also turned down offers to escape. They marched four abreast in the broiling heat, holding high the flag of King Matt, green on one side, with the blue Star of David set against a field of white on the other, escorted by soldiers, whips, and dogs. We learn from the memoir of Nahum Remba, a Judenrat official who ran a small first aid station on the Umschlaplatz, that 4,000 orphans, with their caretakers, went on the transports with Korczak and the children that day. He tried to persuade Korczak to go with him to ask the Judenrat to intercede, but Korczak would not consider leaving the children even for a moment in this terrifying place. Then to Remba's dismay, Schmerling, the sadistic chief of the ghetto police in charge of the Umschlagplatz, ordered that the orphanages be loaded. Korczak led his group in a quiet procession to the train. "I shall never forget this scene as long as I live," Remba wrote. "This was no march to the trains, but rather a mute protest, with eyes full of contempt for this murderous regime."

The Jewish police jumped to attention and saluted when they saw Korczak helping the children into the chlorinated freight cars. The Germans asked: "Who is that man?" The doors closed. There were no survivors.

There is some mystery about how the *Ghetto Diary* was saved. When I met with Igor Newerly at his Warsaw home in 1981, he told me that the day after Korczak and the orphans marched to the trains, a red-haired boy appeared at his door with a package and ran off. Newerly realized that Korczak had kept his promise to send him the diary. He took it immediately to Korczak's Polish orphanage and helped the caretaker brick it up under the eaves. After the war, when Poland was part of the Soviet bloc, Newerly, who had survived two years in Auschwitz (where he thought he spotted the red-haired boy), was able to retrieve the diary from its hiding place. He gave it to the Polish Writers Union. It remained there, unpublished, during the Stalinist years, when Korczak was considered a "bourgeois educator" and the work of the Russian educator Anton Makarenko was favored.

After the thaw of 1956, Newerly, now a famous writer, was able to publish a four-volume anthology of Korczak's writings. The *Ghetto Diary* was included in it. Ida Merzan, a former apprentice in the pre-war Jewish orphanage, helped Newerly mount the delicate blue rice paper on which the manuscript was typed onto heavy cardboard to keep it from disintegrating. This original, laboriously typed manuscript, with many erasures and corrections, has disappeared. The question is: Why?

Both Newerly and Merzan said that the diary had not been edited, except for the deletion of a few names and others that had been replaced with initials. Merzan explained that some of the Jews who held high positions in the Communist government after the war were upset by the critical things Korczak had written about their relatives. Some Polish officials objected to any mention of former patriots like Jozef Pilsudski, who had been anti-Communist. When Merzan tried to locate the original diary, she was told to stop searching, that she would never find it. Still, she believed that after her generation passed on, the original diary would reappear.

A year before the war ended, the captive Jewish workers in charge of unloading the trains to Treblinka burned down most of the camp, and the Nazis completed the destruction to hide their traces. The visitor to Treblinka does not encounter guard towers, barbed wire fences, barracks, empty suitcases, and piles of shoes as in Auschwitz and other camps. Sometime after the war, the violated space that had been Treblinka was transformed into a vast stone garden. Beautiful dense birch and pine forests still line the path to the fake railroad station with the fake clock whose hands never moved, a reminder of the clock in *Senate of Madmen,* which had only one hand—a sword. One follows stone railroad tracks that symbolize the real tracks that led to the death camp. A tall stone monument is dedicated to the Warsaw dead. Seventeen thousand rocks brought in from Polish quarries represent the villages, towns, and countries of the one million men, women, and children who died there—all, except for a thousand gypsies, Jews. Only one rock is engraved: "JANUSZ KORCZAK (HENRYK GOLDSZMIT) AND THE CHILDREN."

Over the years, the Korczak legend has gathered momentum in Europe as poets and playwrights continue to re-create his march with the children to the trains. Korczak societies have sprung up in many countries and hold international conferences to spread his educational ideas and to advocate for the welfare of children. In 1971, the Russians discovered a new asteroid and named it 2163 Korçzak. Now the Old Doctor really does have a planet very much like Planet Ro from which to control the moral forces in the universe and to put into effect his Declaration of Children's Rights.

JANUSZ KORCZAK

GHETTO DIARY

PART ONE

Reminiscences make a sad, depressing literature.

Artists, scholars, politicians and great leaders of men—all of them start out with ambitious plans, resolute actions, aggressive, bold moves. They climb higher and higher, overcome obstacles, extend the range of their influence and, armed with experience and a large number of friends, they press—with increasing ease and success—stage by stage, toward their objective. This takes ten years, sometimes twice, three times that long. And then . . .

Then comes fatigue: bit by bit, still doggedly moving in the once chosen direction—only now along a more leisurely road, with diminished zeal and with a painful realization that their life is not what they had meant it to be, that it is not enough, and especially difficult to face single-handed—they find that the only thing they had achieved is more graying hair, wrinkles on the once smooth and bold forehead, failing eyesight, slower circulation and tired feet.

What has happened? It is old age.

Some will resist, try not to give in, to go on as usual, even at a faster pace and more aggressively, for time is short. They deceive themselves, they fight back, rebel and thrash about. Others, in sad resignation, not only give up but even regress.

"I can't go on. I won't even try. What for? I can no longer understand the world. Ah, to recover the years gone by, reduced to ashes, the strength squandered in blundering, the wasteful momentum of the old zeal . . ."

New people appear, a new generation, new needs.

Now they begin to irritate him, as he irritates them; first there are some misunderstandings, later—lasting lack of understanding. Their gestures, their walk, their eyes, their white teeth and smooth faces, even though their lips are silent . . .

Everything and everyone around you, the entire world, and you yourself, and your stars, keep saying: "This is it . . . Your sun has set . . . Now it is our turn . . ." Your time is over . . . You say we don't know very much . . . We shall not argue with you—you do know more than we do, you're experienced, but you must let us try our own way . . .

Such is the order of life.

So it is with man and animal, so it seems to be with trees, and who knows, perhaps with stones as well.

Today is their will, their power, their time. Yours—today old-age, and the day after tomorrow—decrepitude.

The hands of the clocks move faster and faster.

The stony gaze of the sphinx asks the eternal question:

"Who is it that walks on all fours in the morning, briskly on two legs at noon, and on three in the evening?"

It is you—leaning on your cane, gazing into the dying cold rays of the setting sun. . . .

I shall try to do something different with the story of my own life. Perhaps the idea is good, perhaps it will work, perhaps this is the right way.

When you dig a well, you do not start at the deepest end. First you break up the upper layer, throw the earth aside, shovelful after shovelful, not knowing what is underneath, how many tangled roots, what other obstacles, how many stones forgotten and buried by yourself and by others.

6

The decision is made. There's strength enough to start. And, in fact, is any work ever really finished? Roll up your sleeves. A firm grip on the shovel. Let's go!

One, two; one, two . . .

"God help you, old man! But what's your plan?"

"Can't you see for yourself? I seek subterranean springs; I push aside clear, cool streams of water and browse through the memories."

"May I help you?"

"No, my dear friend, this each man must do alone. Nobody can undertake the job for him or replace him. Everything else we can do together so long as you trust and respect me; but this final work of mine—I must do myself."

"May God help you!"

Now then . . .

I intend to refute a deceitful book by a false prophet. This book has done a great deal of harm.

Also sprach Zarathustra.

And I spoke, I had the honor to speak, with Zarathustra. His wise mysteries, profound, difficult and piercing, have landed you, you poor philosopher, behind the dark walls and the heavy bars of a lunatic asylum, for that is how it was. It says so in black and white:

"Nietzsche died insane, at odds with life!"

In my book I want to prove that he had died painfully at odds with truth.

The very same Zarathustra had taught me something different. But perhaps I had better hearing, perhaps I listened with greater care.

In this much we are together: the road of the master and my own road, the disciple's, were both difficult. There were more defeats than successes, many devia-

7

tions and thus much time and effort wasted, or seemingly wasted.

For in the hour of reckoning I am not inside a solitary cell of the saddest hospital in the world but surrounded by butterflies and grasshoppers, and glowworms, and I hear a concert of crickets and a soloist high up in the sky—the skylark.

Merciful Lord!

Thank you, Merciful Lord, for the meadow and the bright sunsets, for the refreshing evening breeze after a hot day of toil and struggle.

Thank you, Merciful Lord, for having arranged so wisely to provide flowers with fragrance, glowworms with the glow, and make the stars in the sky sparkle.

How joyous old age is.

How delectable the silence.

How sweet the repose.

"Man is so immeasurably blessed with Thy gifts, whom Thou hast created and saved . . ."

Well then. Here I do.

One, two . . .

Two old men sit warming themselves in the sun.

"Tell me, you old codger, how is it that you are still alive?"

"Well, I've led a respectable, sensible life free of shocks and sudden turns. I don't smoke, drink, play cards, chase women. Was never hungry, never too tired, lived without haste and took no risks. With precision and moderation. I did not strain my heart or exhaust my lungs or overtax my brain. Moderation, peace and reflection. That is why I am still alive."

"And how about you, friend?"

"Somewhat differently. Wherever a bruise or a bump on the head was to be found, there I was. As only a young pup, I had my first taste of revolution and shooting. Sleepless nights and enough time in the cooler as would take the rough edges off any youngster. Then the war. I took it as it came. It had to be sought out in remote places, beyond the Ural mountains, beyond Lake Baikal, across the Tatar, Kirghiz, Buryat country, right up to China. I rested for a time in the Manchurian Village of Taoway-jou and—another revolution. Then came peace, of a sort, for a brief while. I drank vodka, to be sure, and more than once staked my life—not just a crumpled bank note—on a single card. But I had no time for girls, although, were it not for the fact they're such a greedy lot and occupy so many of your nights, and besides they do get pregnant . . . A nasty habit. It happened to me once. Left a bad taste in my mouth for life. I had enough of it, the threats and the tears. I smoked cigarettes endlessly. During the day, during any discussion, one after another, like a chimney. And there isn't a bit of me left in sound health. Adhesions, aches, raptures, scars. I am falling to pieces, I groan, I am unstitched, but I'm alive. And how I live! Anyone who has gotten in my way will tell you. I can still kick pretty hard, that you can believe. Even now it happens that a whole gang will slink away when they see me. And I do have followers and friends as well . . ."

"So have I. And children and grandchildren. And you, my friend?"

"Two hundred"

"You like to joke, don't you . . ."

*

It is now the year 1942. The month of May. The month of May is cold this year. And tonight is the quietest of all nights. It is five in the morning. The little ones are a-

9

sleep. There are really two hundred of them. In the east wing—Miss Stefa, and I in the west, in the so-called "solitary."

My bed stands in the middle of the room. Under the bed—a bottle of vodka; on the night table, black bread and a jug of water.

Good old Felek, he has sharpened the pencils at both ends. I could write with a fountain pen; one was given to me by Hadaska, the other by the father of a difficult boy.

I already have a groove impressed in my finger by the pencil. It just now occurs to me that I could do it differently, more conveniently, that a pen is easier.

It was not for nothing that as a child my dad called me a gawk and a clod and, when he flew into rage, even an idiot and an ass. Grannie was the only one who believed in my star. Otherwise all I heard was—lazy, crybaby, idiot (as I've said before), and good-for-nothing.

But more about that later.

They were right. Both equally right. Half grannie, half dad.

But more about that later.

Lazy . . . quite right, I don't like writing. Thinking—yes, definitely. No difficulty. It's like telling myself fairy tales.

Once I read somewhere: "There are people who do not think, in the way that some say 'I don't smoke'."

I do think.

One, two, one, two. I gawk compulsively at each clumsy shovelful from my well. I ponder over it for some ten minutes. And not just because today I'm weak in my old age.

It was always so.

Grannie would give me raisins and say: "You, philosopher."

Allegedly even then, in an intimate chat, I confided to

10

grannie my bold scheme to remake the world. It was—no less, no more—to throw away all money. How and where, and what to do next I probably had no idea. Do not judge me too harshly. I was only five then, and the problem was perplexingly difficult: what to do so there wouldn't be any dirty, ragged and hungry children with whom one was not allowed to play in the backyard (where under a chestnut tree, in a candy box, wrapped in cotton, was buried my first dearly beloved creature, then still only a canary)? Its death had brought about the mysterious question of religion.

I had wanted to put a cross on top of the grave. The housemaid said no, because it was only a bird, something much, much lower than man. Even to cry over it was a sin.

So much for the housemaid. What was worse, the janitor's son decided that the canary was Jewish.

And so was I.

I too was a Jew, and he—a Pole, a Catholic. It was certain paradise for him, but as for me, if I did not use dirty words and never failed dutifully to steal sugar for him from the house—I would end up, when I died, in a place which, though not hell, was nevertheless dark. And I was scared of a dark room.

Death—Jew—hell. A black Jewish paradise. Certainly plenty to think about.

*

I am in bed. The bed is in the middle of the room. My subtenants are: Monius, the younger (we have four of them), then Albert and Jerzyk. On the other side, against the wall, Felunia, Gienia and Haneczka.

The door to the boys' dormitory is open. There are

sixty of them. A bit farther east are sixty girls, peacefully asleep.

The rest are on the top floor. It is May, and although it has been cold the older boys can, in a pinch, sleep in the top-floor hall.

It is night. I have my notes about the night and about the sleeping children. Thirty-four small pads filled with notes. That is why it took me so long to make up my mind to write my memoirs.

I plan to write:

1. A thick volume about the night in an orphanage and about sleeping children in general.

2. A two-volume novel. It takes place in Palestine. The first night of a newly-married Halutz couple at the foot of Mount Gilboa, in a spot where a spring bubbles up; a reference to that mountain and that spring is made in the Book of Moses.

(That well of mine will be a deep one, if I have the time.)

3, 4, 5, 6. Some years ago I wrote a piece for children on the life of Pasteur. And now a continuation of that series: Pestalozzi, da Vinci, Kropotkin, Pilsudski, and a few dozen more, including Fabre, Multatuli, Ruskin and Gregor Mendel, Nalkowski, Szczepanowski, Dygasinski, Dawid.[1]

Ever heard of Nalkowski?

The world knows nothing of many great Poles.

7. Years ago I wrote a novel about King Matthew.

1. Jean-Henri Fabre, French entomologist (1823–1915); Multatuli, pen name of E. D. Dekker, Dutch writer (1820–1887); John Ruskin, English author and critic (1819–1900); Gregor-Johann Mendel, famous Austrian geneticist (1822–1884); Waclaw Nalkowski, eminent Polish geographer, pedagogue and civic leader (1856–1911); Stanislaw Szczepanowski, business promoter, journalist, pioneer of Polish oil industry (1846–1900); Adolf Dygasinski, Polish novelist, storyteller, journalist and pedagogue (1839–1902); Jan Wladyslaw Dawid, Polish psychologist and pedagogue (1858–1914).

Now came the time for the king-child: King David the
Second.

8. Why waste the material of five hundred of the children's weight and height charts and not describe the
wonderful, true, joyous work of the growth of man? In
the coming five thousand years, somewhere in the abyss
of time, there will be socialism; now there is anarchy. A
war of poets and musicians in the most splendid of
Olympic Games. A war for the most beautiful prayer, for
a world hymn to God once a year.

I have forgotten to mention that now, too, a war is
going on.

10. An autobiography.

Yes. About myself, about my little and important self.

Someone once said bitterly that the earth is a speck of
mud suspended in space; and man is an animal who has
made a career.

This may be so. But here's an addendum: this drop of
mud knows what suffering is, it can love and weep and is
full of longing.

And as for man's career, if you consider it carefully,
the issue is highly doubtful.

It is half past six.

In the dormitory someone shouts:

"Boys, time for a bath, get up!"

I put away my pen. Should I or should I not get up? It
is a long time since I have had a bath. Yesterday I caught
on myself and killed without turning a hair—with one
dexterous squeeze of the nail—a louse.

If I have the time, I shall write a eulogy to a louse. For
our attitude toward this fine insect is unjust and unfit-
ting.

An embittered Russian peasant once declared:

"A louse is not like a man, it will not suck up every last drop of blood."

I have written a short tale about sparrows whom I have been feeding for twenty years. I had set for myself the task of exonerating the little thieves. But who will explore the persecution of the louse?

Who if not I?

Who will come forward, who will have the courage to come forward in its defense?

*

"For the callous attempt to shift the responsibility for an orphan onto the shoulders of the community, for the arrogance of the insults, abuses and threats hurled around in a frenzy at the failure of your attempt—you, madam, have to pay within five days 500 zlotys to the "Orphans' Aid" fund.

"Taking into account the low level of your social environment, the house where you live, the fine is set rather low. I expect deceitful excuses that you did not know who it was who conducted the interview; when your youngest progeny, sent to escort me, had seen my identity card shown to the policeman, she shouted in parting: 'animal!'. I did not insist on the young person's arrest, taking into consideration her age and the fact that she was not wearing an armband.[2]

"Finally, allow me to mention that this was my second unhappy encounter with the riff-raff of the elegant house at 14 Walicow Street, for during the siege of Warsaw they refused me help carry a dying soldier, his chest wide open, into the courtyard, so that he might not die like a dog in the gutter."

2. Armband indicating that the child was Jewish.

Here are a few comments:

The lady occupants of the premises from which I was chased away with shouts of: "Get out of here, you old bastard, break your leg and your arm!"—those lady occupants were "friends" of none other than Stefania Sempolowska.[3]

I should like to enlarge of this theme, since the matter has broader implications.

Sempolowska was a fanatical advocate of the Jews, defending us against false as well as justified charges made against us by equally fanatical enemies.

The three Jewesses from Walicow Street—they were the types who by glib talk and, yes, even baptism, would force their way shamelessly into Polish society, into Polish homes and families, there to represent the Jews.

I tried repeatedly, though without effect, to explain to Miss Stefania, the enthusiast, that there could not be, nor ought there be any unison or even as much as casual contact between the Jewish scum and the Polish intellectual, moral elite.

During the thirty years of our association, this precisely was the cause of our deplorable differences and estrangements.

Wojciechowski – Pilsudski – Norwid – Mickiewicz – Kosciuszko – Zajaczek[4], who knows, perhaps Lukasiewicz[5] as well, or even Creon and Antigone—was their remoteness from one another caused precisely by their closeness?

And earlier, Nalkowski and Straszewicz, seemingly enemies, were in fact filled with longing for each other.

3. A well-known author and liberal social worker (1870–1943).

4. Some well-known Poles whom Korczak knew personally, and some historical figures.

5. Jan Lukasiewicz (1878–1956), philosopher, logician, professor at Lwow, Warsaw and Lublin universities.

15

How easy it is for two rogues to get together for joint enterprise in treachery, crime, fraud, but how utterly impossible a harmonious collaboration between two people who love equally well, but with a different understanding of that love, based on a different stock of experience.

I have always hated and detested Jewish peddlers of ideas and platitudes. And I have also witnessed the dignity of those Jews who, having escaped, were in hiding so as not to meet their friends from outside the trenches.

Who could forget dear old "Wojtek," a militant nationalist who, over a cup of coffee, asked almost with despair:

"Tell me, what is one to do? The Jews are digging our grave."

Or Godlewski:

"We are a weak lot. For a glass of vodka, we sell ourselves into Jewish bondage."

Or Moszczenska:

"Your virtues are a death sentence to us."

The corner of Zelazna and Chlodna. A meat shop. Overflowing a chair, an enormously fat Jewess is trying on a pair of shoes. The visiting shoemaker is kneeling in front of her. A sensitive, spiritual face. Gray hair, wise, kind eyes, serious, deep voice, on his face an expression of hopeless resignation.

"But I did warn you that these shoes . . ."

"And I am warning you that you might as well keep these shoes for your wife, mister. Are you a shoemaker, or aren't you, eh? How does it look, that foot of mine?"

And she dangles her fat foot in front of his nose, almost touching it.

"Are you blind? Can't you see how it crinkles?"

One of the worst scenes I have ever witnessed, but not the only one.

16

"Our people are no better."
"I know."
Well then, what's the answer?

*

Radios belong to those who have bought them. So do cars. And theater tickets. And trips, and books, and paintings.

Perhaps I might describe a group of Polish tourists I met in Athens. Taking snapshots of one another in front of, no more, no less, but the Pantheon. Chirping, giggly—but then, every pup turns in circles to catch its own tail.

Why am I writing all this?

Well, yes. The devil does exist. But even among devils some are more and some are less wicked.

*

Little Janusz and Irka built a garden in the sand, and a little house, and flowers, and a picket fence. They carried water in a matchbox. They took turns. Then they conferred: and built another house. Then they conferred: and added a chimney. They conferred: and added a well. They conferred: and added a doghouse.

The dinner bell rang. Moving toward the dining room, they turned back twice to put on the final touches, to have one more look.

All the while Musiek observed from a distance. Then he kicked down the edifice, trampled over it, hit it a long time with his stick.

When they returned after dinner, Irka said:

"I know: it's Musiek."

Born in Paris, he was offered back to his homeland and

17

for three years has been making life impossible for the thirty orphans in the kindergarten.

I wrote an article about him for *Special Pedagogics* advocating penal colonies; I even hinted at death penalty. He is little yet! So he'll be at large for fully fifty years!

Said dear Miss Maria with a perplexed smile:

"You must have been joking?"

"Far from it. How much human misery, how much pain, how many tears . . ."

"So you don't believe in reform?"

"I am not Adler," I said gruffly.

No one can be angry for long with Dr. Maria Grzegorzewska. The compromise: I erased the death penalty— left just the penal colony (and that only with difficulty).

Are decent people in positions of leadership condemned to Calvary for ever and ever?

Why am I writing all this?

*

Of course, it's night. Twelve thirty.

I've had a hard day.

There was the conference with two gentlemen, two high priests of social welfare. Then two interviews, one involving the row referred to earlier. Then a meeting of the Board.

Tomorrow—39 Dzielna Street.

I said to that lawyer:

"Listen, if each day things improve even by a tenth of an inch, it encourages greater effort. If things get worse each day, disaster will come and with it some change. But we are motionless."

Pay attention. What I have to say may come in handy.

There are four ways of dealing with undesirable new-comers:

1. To bribe them. To admit them to your gang and then bamboozle them.

2. To agree to anything and, watching for the moment they are off guard, to go on as usual, doing as you please. I am just one against all the rest. I assess them, at a liberal estimate, about three hours daily. They think around the clock of how to deceive me. I shall explain this when writing about thinking in one's sleep. All this is well known, anyway.

3. To wait, to mark time, lie low and when the right time comes—to discredit them.

"You see! It was his idea!"

One could lie. (They offered to leave the money in my care.)

4. To wear them out. Either they will go away or stop spying. Because why bother?

I've run out of ink.

*

I feel old whenever I reminisce about the past, the bygone years and events. I want to be young, so I make plans for the future.

What shall I do after the war?

Perhaps I will be invited to participate in building a new order in the world, or in Poland. This is highly improbable and I would not want it. I would have to keep an office, meaning the slavery of fixed working hours and contacts with people, a desk somewhere, a telephone, an armchair. Wasting time on current, petty everyday problems and contending with petty people with their petty ambitions, their influential friends, hierarchies and goals.

In sum—a yoke.

I prefer to be on my own.

When I was laid up with the typhus, I had the following vision:

A huge theater or concert hall. Crowds of people, all dressed up.

I am giving an address about war and hunger, orphans and misery.

I speak in Polish. An interpreter translates quickly into English. (All this takes place in America.) Suddenly my voice breaks. There is silence. Somewhere in the hall a cry may be heard. Running toward me is Regina. She stops in front of the dais, throws a watch on the platform and cries out: "For you—everything!" And then there is a shower of bank notes, gold and jewelry. People are tossing their rings, bracelets, necklaces. Boys from the Children's Home come running onto the stage: the Gelblat brothers, Falka, Meir Kulawski, Gluzman, Szejwacz—and they stuff all this into mattresses. The audience, deeply moved, cheer, applaud and weep.

I have no particular faith in prophecies, and yet for well over twenty years I have been waiting for the vision to come true.

I shall have something to say about Regina when I write of the strange fate of the inmates of the white house on Krochmalna Street in Warsaw.[6]

So I shall come into unlimited material means and shall open a contest for the construction of a huge orphanage in the hills of Lebanon, near Kfar Giladi.[7]

It will have large barracks-like dining rooms and dormitories. There will be small "hermit huts." For myself, on the terrace of a flat roof I will have one room, not too

6. Korczak's institution before the ghetto was at 92 Krochmalna Street.
7. A kibbutz in Northern Galilee which Korczak visited during a trip to what is now Israel.

large, with transparent walls, so that I might not miss a single sunrise or sunset and so that, writing at night, I might be able to look now and again at the stars.

Young Palestine is making arduous and honest efforts to come to terms with the earth. But the heaven's turn will also come. Otherwise all would be a misunderstanding, a mistake.

Why not Birobidjan, Uganda, California, Ethiopia, Tibet, Madagascar, India, Southern Russia or Polesie? Even England, well meaning and world-wise, does not know where to plant that handful of Jewry, small as it is.

Every year I should visit for a few weeks my native town, my friends, to talk over important, eternal problems . . .

To be sure, my dream is never monotonously the same. Each time I make certain modifications.

My most serious problem is with the construction of huts for the hermits. Those who have earned a life of solitude aspire to happiness through solitude, they can read it and must translate it into comprehensible language—*orbi et urbi*. They simply must, must, must have it; but what is it they should have? There's the rub.

Once again Moszek has forgotten to put enough carbide in the lamp. The flame is dying.

I must stop now.

Five o'clock in the morning

Good old Albert, he has let the daylight in.

The window panes are covered with black paper shades so that our lights would not interfere with the military authorities' lamp signaling, and they also say they may guide enemy planes. As if there were not enough other signals and landmarks. But folks will believe anything.

So it is light again.

People are naive and good-hearted. And probably un-happy. They have not much of an idea what happiness consists of. Everyone understands it differently.

To some, it's a delicious cholent or sausage with sauer-kraut. To others—peace, comfort, luxury. To still others—women, many and varied, or else—music, or cards, or traveling.

And everyone combats boredom and nostalgia in a different way.

Boredom—a hunger of the spirit.

Nostalgia—a thirst, a thirst for water and for flight, for freedom. And a yearning for a man, a confidant, a confes-sor, an advisor, a yearning for counsel, confession, for an understanding ear to hear my lament.

The spirit feels a longing inside the narrow cage of the body. Man feels and ponders death as though it were the end, when in fact death is merely the continuation of life, it is another life.

You may not believe in the existence of the soul, yet you must acknowledge that your body will live on as green grass, as a cloud. For you are, after all, water and dust.

"The world is the metamorphosis of evil, everlasting"—Tetmajer[8] has said.

This unbeliever, pessimist, nihilist, he too speaks of eternity.

The amoeba is immortal, and man is a colony of sixty trillion amoebas—said Maeterlinck. And he knew the experts. Because, for a dozen odd years I have tried unsuccessfully to find out how many times to multiply two billion—the population of the world.

8. Polish poet, novelist, playwright, representative of "Young Poland" (1865–1940).

My fellow teacher, Professor Paszkiewicz, said the figure was astronomical. Until by chance I found the answer in Maeterlinck's *Termites*.

There are two billion people in the world, and I constitute a community many million times greater, therefore I have the right, I have the duty to look after my own trillions toward which I have certain responsibilities.

Perhaps it is not safe to tell the general public about this, although everyone must sense it anyway, even if not altogether consciously. Anyhow, is my own universe and its fate not related to the fate of my entire generation, from the Australian cannibal islands to the workshop of a poet, a scientist looking through his telescope set on a snowbound peak or a polar plain?

When little Genka coughs during the night, in an altruistic sense I feel pity for her, but egoistically I weigh the disturbance in the night, the concern for her health against: maybe she's contagious? the expense of the extra food, the trouble and the costs involved in sending her to the country.

I feel sleepy. Before my beehive begins to buzz, I shall try to nap for an hour.

I am convinced that in a future rational society the dictatorship of the clock will come to an end. To sleep and eat when you feel like it.

How lucky that the doctors and the police cannot prescribe how many times I may be allowed to breathe per minute, how many times my heart has the right to beat.

I do not like to sleep at night because then I cannot sleep in the daytime. Bread and water taste better at night.

It is nonsense to put a child to bed for ten hours of uninterrupted sleep.

The man of the future will be astonished to find that

JANUSZ KORCZAK / GHETTO DIARY

we used cut flowers to decorate our apartments. And hung paintings on our walls. And used animal skins for carpets.

They are scalps, scalps of flowers and scalps of our noble younger brothers, the animals.

And the canvas, smeared with colors, which one does not even see after a time, with dust settling on the frame and vermin on the back . . .

How petty, savage and miserable was that primitive man of thousands of years ago!

And they will lament over our primitive systems of education.

What stifling ignorance of the lifeless language!

When associating with "the simple folk," now and then I would fish out talent among the children.

Somewhere in Solec, in a laborer's shack, I came across some sketches drawn by a small boy: a horse was a horse, a tree was a tree, a ship was a ship.

I took a roll of the drawings, those that seemed to me to be the best, to show to a well-known painter.

He examined them and said with a grimace:

"It's absolutely worthless. Copies. Only this one, perhaps, is passable."

And then he said something odd:

"Everyone should know how to sketch in pencil what he wants to retain in memory. Not to be able to do that is to be illiterate."

How often did I recollect this irrefutable truth.

Here is a scene, a face, a tree, but in a moment they will be lost to me forever. What a shame, what a pity!

The tourists have found a way: the photograph. And now even film. A generation of children and young people is growing up today who will be able to watch their own first clumsy steps.

The unforgettable sight of the dormitory coming

24

awake: A sleepy gaze, languid motions, or a sudden leaping out of bed. One of them rubs his eyes, another wipes the corners of his mouth with the sleeve of his nightshirt, still another strokes his ear, stretches, or holding an article of clothing in his hand stares motionless into space.

Energetically or phlegmatically, skillfully or clumsily, with self-assurance or timidly, with precision or carelessly, deliberately or mechanically.

These are real tests: you can sum him up at a glance, who he is and why he always acts this way, or if not, why today.

A lecturer provides commentary to a film:

"Look carefully, please (he points with a cane, as though to a map). A resentful exchange of glances between the two on the right shows their mutual dislike; their beds should not be adjacent.

"The squinting eyes of this one prove conclusively that he is nearsighted.

"Do not trust the endurance of this boy over here: he shows strain, nervousness of movements, a variable rhythm, interruptions in his seemingly steady haste. Perhaps he has taken on a wager, has challenged to a race that boy on the left, the one at whom he keeps glancing.

"And for this one I predict a bad day today. Something is wrong with him. While washing, making his bed, at breakfast, very soon, or in an hour, he will get into an argument or a fight, or will talk back to the teacher."

We were standing, the two of us, by the window while a new game of "two fires" was about to be organized.

A noble, chivalrous game.

A ten-year-old expert was my instructor:

"He'll get a beating right off, because he's tired. And that one'll show what he can do halfway through the game, as soon as he tries harder. This one will be thrown out. See that one, he's got eyes in the back of his head, looks to the right and passes to the left. This one will surrender, sneakily, to cut out those other two later on. And that one will get mad, quarrel and cry."

Should the forecast prove wrong, the expert knows exactly why and explains. In his calculations and assessment of the situation, he has failed to take this or that into account:

"He's playing this way because yesterday he broke a window and now he's scared. That one's got the sun in his eyes and that other one hasn't gotten used to the ball, it's too hard for him. A sore foot—that one. This wonderful shot's his friend's doing—always backs him up!"

He reads the game like a musician reads the score, commenting on the moves as if it were a game of chess.

If I have a vague idea about it all, I owe it to my devoted instructors. How patient, selfless, friendly they are; what a slow, inept student I am.

No wonder: I was over forty when soccer appeared in this country, while these boys crawled on all fours holding a ball under the arm.

Five thick volumes:
1. Plain ball.
2. Soccer.
3. "Two fires."
4. The psychology and philosophy of ball playing.
5. Life stories, interviews. Descriptions of outstanding shots, games, stadiums.

And a hundred kilometers of film.

If I have anticipated a reaction well in advance then nothing irritates me, makes me impatient or angry.

Today the class will be restless because it's April Fool's Day, because it's hot, because in three days there's to be an outing, because the holidays are in a week, because I've got a headache.

I remember a school teacher, already experienced in the profession, who would get indignant at the boys because their hair grew so fast. And I remember a young boarding-school worker, a beginner, who used to start her routine report on the girls' bedtime with:

"Tonight the girls were impossible. At nine they were still talking. At ten, still whispering and laughing. And all this because the principal had me on the carpet, because I was angry, because I was in a hurry, because tomorrow I have an exam, because I mislaid my stockings, because I've received a disturbing letter from home."

Someone will say:

"What is a film worth if the children know they are being filmed?"

Easy:

The camera is fixed in one place. The operator turns the handle with no film in the camera, at different times and angles. The children are promised they will see the film when it's ready, but every time something seems to go wrong. Sequences are repeatedly taken of troublesome, difficult, unpopular children and uninteresting happenings. The children are never once told to be natural, to look this way and not that way or to "act normally." The floodlights are switched on and off at random. Then again a game is interrupted and a grueling rehearsal ordered.

After a period of initial fascination comes impatience. Finally, they cease to take any notice. After a week, a month. But why bother explaining it? Certainly it is done like that. There's no other way.

A teacher who does not know this is an illiterate, a fool if he does not understand it.

In the future, every teacher will have to be a stenographer and a cameraman.

And dictaphones, and the radio?

And the epoch-making experiments of Pavlov?

Or the horticulturist who by crossbreeding and grafting has grown roses without thorns and "pears on willow trees"?[9]

We do already have a basic sketch of a man—perhaps even a photograph? Perhaps we're not far off? All that's needed is skillful and conscientious retouching.

Others are afraid to sleep in the daytime in order not to spoil the night. It's the reverse with me. I sleep at night unwillingly—I prefer the daytime.

May 15, six o'clock

I already know about the girls half of what I ought to know.

It went something like this. A question:

"You know, Helcia, you're a restless person."

She:

"I am a person?"

"Why, of course. You're not a puppy."

She pondered. After a long pause, surprised:

"I am a person. I am Helcia. I am a girl. I am Polish. I am mummy's little daughter. I am a Warsaw inhabitant . . . What a lot of things I am!"

And again:

"I have a mummy, a daddy, a grannie, two grannies, a granddaddy, a dress, hands, a doll, a little table, a canary, an apron. And do I have you?"

A certain nationalist told me:

"A Jew, a sincere patriot, is at best a 'Warsawer' or 'Cracower', but not a Pole."

9. A Polish saying corresponding to achieving the impossible. (Transl.)

I was rather taken aback.

I did admit frankly that I am unmoved by Lwow, Poznan, Gdynia, the Augustow Lakes or Zaleszczyki, as well as the Zaolzie region. I have never been to Zakopane (what a monster.) I am not drawn to Polesie, the seashore or the Bialowieza Forest. The river Vistula near Cracow is alien to me. I don't know and don't want to know Gniezno. But I love the Warsaw Vistula, and when cut off from Warsaw I feel fiercely nostalgic.

Warsaw is mine and I am Warsaw's. I'll say more—I am her. Together with her I have rejoiced and I have grieved, her weather was my weather, her rain, her soil mine as well. We grew up together. Lately, we have grown apart to some extent. New streets, new sections have been built which I no longer understood. For years now I've felt like a foreigner at Zoliborz.[10] I feel closer even to Lublin, even to Hrubieszow which I have never seen.

Warsaw has been my workshop; here are my landmarks and my graves.

I recollect a Nativity play from Freta Street and a small puppet show group from Miodowa Street. It was like this:

Beginning at Christmas, construction workers, unemployed at that time of year, used to go from house to house in the wealthier quarters of the city, and when invited inside homes, would put on a show.

A wooden box for a stage, an accordion or a street organ. And up on the stage—puppets: king Herod on the throne, the devil with a pitchfork.

The show was usually presented in the kitchen so that mud should not be carried from the street to the living room. The cook would put away smaller items so they wouldn't be stolen. On one occasion, two silver spoons

10. A new section of Warsaw.

from a set had disappeared. But the whole thing was beautiful, and scary, and instructive.

When it was over, an old man with a sack appeared to take up collection.

Father always told me to drop the small new silver coins into the old man's sack, and I for my part would change all the cash I had into tiny two-penny coins and, trembling with excitement, toss them into the sack. And the old man would peer inside, shake his long white beard and say:

"Very little, very little, young gentleman, a bit more."

At that time my father took me to a Nativity play.

I recall the long hall of the orphanage, the curtain, the air of mystery, the crowded seats, the expectation.

There were some odd creatures dressed in blue aprons and white caps wearing stiff angels' wings.

I was scared. I was choking with tears.

"Don't go away, daddy."

"Don't be afraid."

A mysterious, strange lady told me to sit in the front row.

Don't ever do that if a child does not want it. I would have much rather sat somewhere to the side, even if others got between me and the stage, even if I was to be crushed and uncomfortable.

Helplessly:

"Daddy!"

"Stay there, silly boy!"

On the way over, I kept asking whether Herod and the devil would be there.

"Wait and see."

This kind of adult reticence is a terrible thing. Don't force surprises on the children if they don't want them. They should be told beforehand, be warned if there's to be any shooting, and if so then when and what kind.

30

After all, a long, dangerous journey requires preparation.

Only one thing is on the adults' mind:

"Don't forget to peepee before we go, you can't go over there."

But I happen to be busy just now, and I don't want to, anyway. I simply can't do it "just in case."

I knew this would be somehow a more important mystery show and a hundred times more marvelous, even without the old man with a sack taking collections.

Better, in fact, without the old man.

As I have said, it was an instructive hour. Yes. The old man. And not only the old man, but he in particular.

He was insatiable.

Into his sack went first the less important parental coins, then my own, laboriously saved coppers. Taught by bitter, degrading experience, I saved them up for a long time in any way I could. Often a real old beggar in the street suffered because of this, as I thought to myself:

"I won't give it to him, I'll save it for my old man with the sack in the Nativity play."

That old man was insatiable, and his sack bottomless. The sack was very little, a fifth of the size of my purse, yet it absorbed, devoured, wrought out every last penny.

I gave and gave, and I tried again, to see if maybe finally he'd say—enough.

Daddy! Granny! Catherine, I'll pay you back, please lend me a few coins! I'll give you my whole year's allowance.

I was curious. Perhaps I'd be able to catch him disappear for a moment behind the stage and then go on to insist and collect again.

And I was worried and upset by the sad realization

that after the old man there comes the end of the play, that there's nothing more.

Worse: that there's the wearisome ritual of washing before going to bed, maybe even cod-liver oil? On such very special days children should be spared some duties, and not be irritated by all the things that history, study, experience have appropriately advised for the benefit of children. They should have a day's vacation.

Total concentration, total freedom, a complete fairy-tale world woven into a drab existence.

The old man from the puppet show on Miodowa Street—a street so dreadfully changed after the siege of Warsaw—had taught me a great deal. The hopelessness of defense against persistent request and unbounded demands that are impossible to meet.

At first, you give eagerly, then less enthusiastically, from a sense of duty, then, following the laws of inertia, from habit and without heart, and then resentfully, angrily, with despair.

And he wants all that is yours, and you yourself as well.

I hold on to the old man in the puppet show as a last thread linking me with that enchanting fairy tale, with the splendid mysteries of life, the magic of the high-colored, festive thrills.

All this is gone—forever. Finished—buried. That special one, that peculiar [. . .] And this his frightening. The good, the evil.

The ardent desire, impotence, multiplicity, nothingness.

Perhaps I can tell you now how I fed sparrows forty years later.

Don't refuse a child if he asks you to tell the same story over and over and over again.

To many children, more perhaps than we realize, a performance should consist of one theme repeated time after time.

A single spectator is frequently a large and responsive audience. Your time will not be wasted.

Old nannies and construction workers are often better pedagogues than a doctor of psychology.

And indeed, the adults, too, cry "Encore!" Encore!

The same fairy tale endlessly repeated, like a sonata, a favorite sonnet, like a sculpture without the sight of which the day seems colorless.

Picture galleries are quite familiar with the phenomenon of a maniac on the subject of some particular item in an exhibit.

Mine are *San Juan* by Murillo at the Vienna Museum and two sculptures in Cracow by Rygier—*Craft* and *Art*.

Before one slips to the very bottom and becomes reconciled to the shoddy nature of one's emotions . . . one struggles, suffers . . . feels ashamed to be different, inferior to the rest of the crowd, or perhaps only painfully experiences one's own loneliness and alienation?

A puppet show without the old man, not a puppet show but a Nativity play.

It was bad, very bad.

Quite rightly mother was reluctant to entrust her children to the care of her husband, and quite rightly, with a thrill of delight and whoops of joy, we welcomed and long remembered—my sister and I—even the most strenuous, exhausting, unfortunate and deplorable in their outcome "pleasures" sought out with an amazing intuition by that not particularly reliable pedagogue—my father.

He pulled our ears painfully, despite the most emphatic protests from mother and grannie.

"If the child goes deaf, it'll be your doing."

*

The hall was unbearably hot. The preparations dragged on indefinitely . . . The faint sounds and whispers coming from behind the curtain put our nerves on the very edge of endurance. The lamps were smoking. The children pushed and shoved.

"Move over! Take that hand away! Keep your legs to yourself. Don't lean on me."

The bell. And then eternity. The bell. Such feelings might be experienced by a pilot under attack when he has run out of ammunition but has still an important assignment to fulfill. There is no going back and no will, desire or thought of going back.

I don't think the analogy is out of place.

It had begun. Something unrepeatable, unique, final.

I have no recollection of the people. I don't even know whether the devil was red or black. Black, more likely, and he had a tail and horns. He was not a puppet. A live devil. Not a child in disguise.

A child in disguise?

Only grownups could believe in such childish stories.

King Herod himself addresses him as:

"Satan!"

And such a laugh, such leaps, and a real tail, and such "No!" and such a pitchfork, and such "Come here!" I have never seen, never heard before and I even suspected, which may well be true, that hell does really exist.

Everything was authentic. The lights go off, there's cigarette smoke, coughing—that is disturbing.

Miodowa and Freta Streets. And on Freta stood Szmurlo's school. There they used the switch on the children. That too was authentic. But absolutely without comparison.

*

Four o'clock

I have drawn the curtain open in one window only, so as not to wake up the children.

Reginka has *erythema nodozum*.[11]

Probably unwisely I have administered today salicylate 10.0 per 200.0, a tablespoonful every two hours, until she heard ringing in the ears and saw yellow. But yesterday she vomited twice. The lumps on her legs, however, are turning pale, small and no longer hurt.

I have a dread of anything connected with rheumatism in children.

Salicylate—so they said in Paris—and who: no less than Hutinel, Marfan and, oddly enough, Baginski in Berlin.[12]

Never mind the vomiting. But enough to bring the unfortunate doctor back again if, of course, he says that this is caused by the medication.

As for me, after the Nativity play I had fever for only a couple of days. And in fact only one night. The fever was not perhaps so high but was emphasized sharply by my mother so that a determined "No!" could be administered at least until spring should father care to bring home ice cream.

I am not certain whether on our way back we did not stop to have ice cream or soda ice with pineapple juice.

11. Rheumatic rash.
12. All three well-known pediatricians of France and Germany.

Artificial ice was not yet known at the time and natural ice was easily available in wintertime. So we were able to cool off after the heat.

I remember that I had lost my scarf.

And I also remember that while I was still in bed for the third day and my father came over toward me, my mother admonished him sternly:

"Your hands are cold. Don't come near him!"

Withdrawing meekly, father threw me a conspiratorial glance.

I answered with a cunning, knowing grin, corresponding to something like:

"Sure thing."

I think we both felt that in the last resort not they—mother, grannie, the cook, sister, the maid and the governess, Miss Maria, that stern regiment of women—hold the upper hand, but we, the men.

We are the masters. But we give in for the sake of peace.

Curiously, during my rather long but not particularly varied practice as a doctor, I was frequently called in by the fathers. But never more than once.

Now the mothers were giving in for the sake of peace.

Let me still tell the story of [. . .]

A comment, or rather a hint, to those who some thirty years from now will be drawing up radio programs:

Devote one hour, half to the grandson, half to the grandfather (or father)—to let them chat about "My day yesterday," "How I spent my day yesterday." The beginning would always be the same:

"Yesterday I woke up at . . . I got up . . . Got dressed."

These chats would teach how to view, how to articulate current events, how to eliminate and how to emphasize, how to experience life, how to evaluate it and treat it lightly, to attack it and to succeed—how to live.

Actually, why not also have talks between women, between a teacher and a pupil, a workman and his employer, a clerk and his customer, a lawyer and his client?

It requires experimentation.

Epilogue.
The Polish language knows no such word as "homeland." Fatherland is too much and it is difficult.

Is one only a Jew or perhaps a Pole as well? Perhaps not fatherland but a little house with a garden?

Does not a peasant love his fatherland?

It's just as well that my pen has almost run dry. I have a hard day ahead of me.

Postscript

Ugolino-Dante. They're all right, I suppose. The puppet show . . . If they were alive, they'd know what's right.

There were years when I kept mercuric chloride and morphine pills hidden in the far corner of a drawer. I would take them out only when I went to my mother's grave at the cemetery. But since the start of the war, I have kept them in my pocket, and it's interesting that they were not confiscated when I was searched in jail.

There can be nothing (no experience) more loathsome than an unsuccessful attempt at suicide. This sort of plan should be fully matured so as to ensure absolute certainty of success.

If I kept on postponing my otherwise fully thought-out

plan, it was because always at the very last moment some new daydream would sweep me away and could not be abandoned before I worked it out in detail. These were something like themes for short stories. I put them under a common heading of: "Oddities".

Thus:

I invented a machine (I made a detailed design of the whole complicated mechanism). Something in the nature of a microscope. The scale—one hundred. If I should turn the micrometer screw to ninety-nine, everything would die that did not contain at least one percent of humanity. The amount of work was unbelievable. I had to determine how many people (living beings) would go out of circulation each time, who would take their place, and what would be the outcome of such a purged, tentative new life. After a year's deliberations (at night, of course) I came half way with the distillation. Now the only people left were half-beasts, all others have perished. How minutely, to the last detail I planned everything—the best proof that my own person was completely excluded from this peculiar system. By a mere turn of the micrometer screw of my "microscope" I could have taken my own life. What then?

I confess with some embarrassment that I return to this theme today, too, on the more difficult nights. Nights in prison have produced the most interesting chapters of my tale.

There was about a dozen of these daydreams in the workshop to choose from.

Thus . . .

I have found the magic word. I am the ruler of light.

I would fall asleep so full of mental anguish that a protest would rise within me.

"Why me? What do you want of me? There are others,

younger, wiser, more pure, more suitable for this mission?

Leave me to the children. I'm not a sociologist. I'll mess up everything, disgrace both the project and myself."

For rest and relaxation I moved to the children's hospital. The city is casting children my way, like little sea shells—and I am just good to them. I ask neither where they come from, nor for how long or where they are going, for good or evil.

The "Old Doctor" doles out candy, tells stories, answers questions. Dear, tranquil years remote from the tawdry marketplace of the world.

A book, a visit from a friend—and always some patient who needs particular care for several years.

Children recover, or die—as always in a hospital.

I did not philosophize. I did not try to analyze a topic which I already knew through and through. Indeed, for the first seven years I was simply a modest resident physician in a hospital. But for the rest of my years I was bothered by the unpleasant feeling that I had deserted. I had betrayed the sick child, medicine and the hospital. I was carried away by false ambition: to become a doctor and a sculptor of the child's soul. The soul. No more, no less. (Oh, you old fool, you've messed up your life and your cause! You got what you deserved!) A woman, a hysterical slob with the mentality of a charwoman, now represents this important sphere of life, and a *maître d'hôtel* dabbles in hygiene.

Is this why I struggled, often hungry, through the clinics of three European capitals? Ah, what's the use.

*

I don't know how much of this autobiographical stuff

I've already scribbled down. I cannot bring myself to read it and examine the overload. And I'm increasingly in danger of repeating myself. What's even worse, the facts and experiences may be, must be and will be told differently each time as regards the details.

But never mind. It only proves that the moments to which I constantly return were experienced deeply.

And it proves that reminiscences hinge on our immediate experience. Reminiscing, we lie unconsciously. This is an obvious fact and I mention it only for the benefit of the most primitive reader.

One of my frequent daydreams and plans was a trip to China.

This could have materialized, even quite easily.

My poor four-year-old Iuo-Ya from the Japanese war period. I wrote a dedication for her in Polish.

She was extraordinarily patient in teaching Chinese to an inept pupil.

Indeed, there ought to be institutes of Oriental languages. Yes, and professors and lectures.

But everyone would have to spend a year in this kind of village in the Orient and pursue a preliminary course of study under a four-year old.

My German was taught to me by Erna. Walter and Friede were already too old for that, already too grammatical, influenced by novels, textbooks, the school.

Dostoyevski says that with time all our dreams come true, only in such degenerated form that we don't recognize them. I can now recognize my dream of the prewar years.

Not that I went to China. China came to me. Chinese famine, Chinese orphan misery, Chinese mass child mortality.

I do not want to dwell on that subject. To describe

someone else's pain resembles thieving, preying upon misfortune, as if there were not enough of it as things are.

The first newsmen and officials from America did not hide their disappointment: things are not *that* bad. They were looking for corpses and skeletons in the orphanages.

When they visited the Children's Home, the boys were playing at soldiers. With paper caps and sticks.

"Obviously the war hasn't upset them too much," said one ironically.

"That's the way it is now. But the appetites have increased and the nerves have grown numb; something is happening at last. Here and there you can see even toys in the shop windows and so much candy—from ten groszy up to a whole zloty."

"I saw it with my own eyes: a tiny tot scrounged ten groszy and promptly spent it on candy."

"Don't put that in your newspaper."

I've read somewhere: nothing is easier to get used to than the misfortune of others.

When we marched to East Prussia through Ostroleka[13] a woman shopkeeper asked us:

"What's going to happen to us civilians? There's no reason why we should suffer. It's different for you officers, you know you're going to certain death."

Only once did I ride in a rickshaw in Harbin. Now in Warsaw, I recoiled from it for a long time.[14]

A rickshaw runner does not live more than three years, a strong one—five.

I didn't want to have any hand in it.

13. During World War I.
14. Korczak refers to the use of man-drawn vehicles in Warsaw during World War II.

But now I say:

"One must help them earn a living. Better I than two fat profiteers with packages in the bargain."

It is an unpleasant moment when I try to pick the healthier, the stronger-looking (when I'm in a hurry). I always give fifty groszy more than what they ask.

How noble—then and now.

When sharing a room with the healthy children, whenever I lit a cigarette I told myself:

"Smoke is a good expectorant. It's good for them."

*

Five glasses of raw alcohol mixed half and half with hot water gives me inspiration.

Then comes a blissful feeling of weariness without pain, when the scar no longer counts, and neither does the muscle ache in the legs, or even the sore eyes and the burning in the scrotum.

I draw my inspiration from the awareness that I'm lying in bed and so I will remain until morning. Thus for twelve hours the lungs, heart and mind will work normally.

After a busy day.

A taste of sauerkraut and garlic in my mouth, and of the candy I've put in the glass with the spirits to make it more palatable. An epicurean!

And that's not all! Two teaspoons of real coffee grounds with ersatz honey.

The odors: ammonia (urine decomposes quickly now, and I don't rinse the bucket every day), the smell of garlic, of carbide and from time to time of one of my seven roommates.

I feel content, calm and safe. Of course, the tranquillity may be disturbed by Miss Stefa coming in with some piece of news, a problem, a desperate decision.

Or by Miss Esterka, to tell me that someone is crying and can't fall asleep because of a toothache. Or Felek, about a letter to that dignitary which has to go out first thing in the morning.

Just now a moth has flown by, and all at once, anger, inner ferment. Bedbugs—the once infrequent visitors—and now moths, our most recent enemies, let's say enemies number five, but, damn it, that's a subject for tomorrow. Now, in the silence of the night (ten o'clock), I want to go over this day. A busy workday, as I've said.

Apropos of vodka: it was the last half-liter bottle from the old allotment. I did not intend to open it. Kept it for a rainy day. But Satan never sleeps—the sauerkraut, the garlic, the need for consolation, and five decagrams of sausage.

It's so peaceful and safe. Yes, even safe. I don't expect any visit from the outside. Of course, there may chance such a visitor as fire, air-raid, or plaster falling from the ceiling. But the very definition "sense of safety" shows that subjectively I take myself as living deep behind the front lines. He who has no knowledge of the front lines will not understand this.

I feel content and I want to write for a long time, until the pen runs dry. Let's say until one, and then have six full hours of rest.

It even makes one want to joke.

"All's fine," said a not quite sober cabinet minister at not quite the right moment because famine and typhus were ravaging throughout the villages and the graph of fatal tuberculosis cases was rising sharply.

Afterward, political opponents picked on him in the pages of newspapers which call themselves independent.

"All's fine," I say, and it's my wish to be merry.

An amusing reminiscence:

Five decagrams of so-called smoked sausage now costs 1 zloty 20. It used to cost only 80 grosze (and bread a bit more).

I said to a saleswoman:

"Tell me, dear lady, isn't that sausage by chance made from human flesh? It's rather too cheap for horsemeat."

And she replied:

"How should I know. I wasn't there when it was being made."

No sign of annoyance, no friendly smile for a witty customer, no shrug to denounce the joke as nightmarish, macabre. Nothing. She merely stopped slicing, waiting for me to make up my mind. A sorry customer, a sorry joke or implication, not worth talking about.

The day began with weighing the children. The month of May has brought a marked decline. The previous months of this year were not too bad and even May is not yet alarming. But we still have two months or more before the harvest. No getting away from that. And the restrictions imposed by official regulations, new additional interpretations and overcrowding are expected to make the situation still worse.

The children's weighing hour on Saturday is one of big excitement.

After breakfast comes the school meeting.

Breakfast itself also amounts to work. It seems that, following my nasty letter to the dignitary, we have received a fairly good supply of sausage, even ham, even a hundred buns.

Never enough, but although it doesn't amount to much "per head" it has an effect.

Then, even a surprise in the form of two hundred kilograms of potatoes.

An echo of the letters. But there is a rub to it. A passing diplomatic victory, an easily won concession should not give rise to exaggerated hopes and lull vigilance.

They will try one way or another to get their own back—how to stop them? From where will the clouds roll in? What invisible ohms, volts, neons will add up into a thunderclap, into an approaching desert wind, and when?

The gnawing: "Have I done right or wrong?" A gloomy accompaniment to the children's carefree breakfast.

After breakfast, on the run, *à la fourchette*—the toilet (just in case, therefore a bit of a struggle), and a meeting to discuss the school's summer program of leaves and substitutes.

It would be convenient if it could be arranged the same way as last year. But a lot has changed since, a different situation in the dormitories, many newcomers and departures, new promotions, things are—why keep on about it—different. And we would like things to be better.

After the meeting, the school newspaper and court decisions. Thefts have occurred. Not everyone is willing to listen carefully for a good hour to the subject of who has managed well and who badly, what has been received and what is missing, what to expect, what to do. The school newspaper will be a revelation to the new children.

But the oldtimers know that in no way will they learn that which is important, most important to them. In fact, no one is interested, no one listens, so why bother?

Immediately after the newspaper, tiring for me who can reasonably acquiesce in and cunningly turn a blind

45

eye to what is more convenient not to see, when one will not use violence if persuasion is impossible—immediately after the newspaper, a longish conversation with a lady using her influence to get a child admitted. This is an intricate business, calling for caution, pleasantness and firmness. You can go absolutely crazy. But about that some other time. The gong has sounded for dinner.

Whether this Saturday's dinner differs in any way from others I'm not sure, so I prefer to put that off, too.

I am planning for today only three addresses and three calls. Looks easy.

1. To call on a supporter after his illness.

2. A talk on yeast for children in a house almost next door.

3. Close by, a welcome to returnees from the east, kind, friendly people whom I wish well.

That's about it, ha . . .

The first call was to amount to a continuation of the morning discussions on the school.

He wasn't home.

"Please convey my belated greetings. I intended to come sooner, but couldn't make it."

One gets tired of thinking—too many thoughts.

And that elderly man, odd and atypical as primary school teacher; what do I know about him? We've not had a longer talk, or maybe no talk of any kind for a whole year.

There wasn't time? I'm lying. (I can no longer keep my eyes open. I can't, really. I'll wake up and finish it later.

. . . Welcome—the beautiful silence of the night.)

I did not wake up, and in the morning letters had to be written.

Continued the next night

Blessed be peace and quiet.

Nota bene. Last night only seven Jews were shot, the so-called Jewish Gestapo men. What can this mean? It's pointless to delve into it.

An hour's lecture on yeast. Brewers' or bakers', active or inactive? How long it should set? How much to take a week and how often?

Vitamin B.

We shall need five liters per week. But how? Through whom? From where?

A lecture on national foods—during the third call. How kugel and cholent were made in his childhood.

An explosion of the old man's reminiscences. It seems that they returned from hell to the Warsaw paradise.

Why not.

"You're just a kid yourself, in age and experience. You don't know anything."

And then the cholent.

Many a time while in Kiev I remembered the tripe, Warsaw style, and wept from longing for my homeland.

He listened and nodded.

At the front entrance I was stopped by the janitor of the house.

"Help, Almighty! Don't let them question us, ask us anything, tell anything."

The body of a dead boy lies on the sidewalk. Nearby, three boys are playing horses and drivers. At one point they notice the body, move a few steps to the side, go on playing.

Anyone who is a little better off must help his family. A family means his and his wife's brothers and sisters, their brothers, sisters, old parents, children. They give between five and fifty zlotys—and so it goes, day in, day out.

If someone is starving and happens to find relatives willing to acknowledge kinship and ensure two meals a day, he will be happy for two or three days, not more than a week, he will then ask for a shirt, shoes, a decent place to live, some coal. Then medical treatment for himself, his wife and children. Finally—he does not want to be a beggar—he demands employment, a steady job.

It cannot be otherwise, yet it makes one so angry, discouraged, apprehensive and disgusted that even a decent and sensitive man turns against family, all men and himself.

I wish I had nothing, so that they might see it for themselves, and that would be that.

I returned utterly shattered from the "rounds." Seven calls, conversations, staircases, questions. The result: fifty zlotys and a promise of five zlotys a month. To provide for two hundred people!

I stretched out on the bed with my clothes on. The first hot day. I cannot sleep, and at nine a so-called educational session. Occasionally someone will burst out, then withdraw (not worthwhile). Occasionally a meek comment (just for the sake of appearances). The ceremony lasts for an hour. Formality has been satisfied from nine to ten. I exaggerate, of course.

I have special thoughts to fall asleep by. This time: what I could eat without the slightest difficulty, without forcing myself.

Astonishing! I, who only six months ago didn't know

exactly what tasted good (some times that which has pleasant associations).

Raspberries (aunt Magdzia's garden), tripe (Kiev), buckwheat groats (father), kidneys (Paris).

In Palestine, I used to soak every dish in vinegar.

And now, for a soothing subject, what should I have?

The answer:

Champagne with dry biscuits and ice cream with red wine.

A harking back to the time of my throat troubles and no ice cream for twenty years. I drank champagne perhaps three times in my life. Dry biscuits I probably ate as a child when ill.

I put a question to myself:

Perhaps fish with Tartar sauce?

A Wiener schnitzel?

Pâté, rabbit marinated in Malaga with red cabbage.

No! A thousand times no!

Why?

Odd: eating is work, and I am tired.

Sometimes, on waking up in the morning, I think:

"To get up, is to sit on the bed, reach for my underpants, button up, if not all the buttons, then at least one. Struggle into my shirt. Bend down to put on my socks. The suspenders. . . ."

I can sympathize with Krylov who spent all his adult years on a couch, with all his books under it. He would reach for and read the first thing that came to his hand.

I can understand the mistress of P., a friend of mine. She never lit a lamp in the evening but used to read by the light of wax matches which he bought her especially for the purpose.

I have a cough. It's hard to work. To step from the sidewalk down to the street, and then climb up again. A passer-by pushed me inadvertently: I staggered to one side and leaned against a wall.

It's not feebleness. I could easily lift a schoolboy, thirty kilograms of living, resistant weight. It's not strength that's lacking but will. As with a cocaine addict. I have even been wondering if there is not something in the tobacco, the raw vegetables, the air we inhale. For I'm not the only one affected. Sleepwalkers—morphine addicts.

The same with memory.

It happens that I'm on my way to see somebody on important matters. And I stop on the landing:

"What did I come to see him about?" I ponder deeply for some time, and then, with relief: "Oh, yes, I remember. (Kobryner—sickness allowance, Herszaft—extra food rations, Kramsztyk—poor quality of coal and its ratio to the quantity of wood.")

Likewise at meetings. The continuity of discussion is easily broken. Someone interrupts with a remark—and we go off at a tangent for a long time.

What was it we were talking about?

Occasionally, somebody starts off with:

"Firstly. . . ."

You wait in vain for: "Secondly."

Of course, some of us are long-winded, anyway.

A motion:

"The child should be admitted."

Recorded: "Admit." We ought to pass to the next application. No. Not one but three speakers support the motion. At times, it is necessary to intervene more than once.

The discussions keep on "skidding" like a badly driven car.

Wearying, irritating.

Enough!

That's just it: enough! There's no such feeling at the front lines. The front line means orders.

"Ten miles forward, five back—halt—countermarch, bivouac here."

On horseback or a motorcycle—day or night—a brief order penciled on a scrap of paper. It must be carried out, no argument.

Only five undamaged houses left in the village.

Prepare to receive two hundred wounded. They're on their way. Get on with it as best you can.

Here, things are different:

"Please, I'd be so grateful. Would you be so kind?"

You're free not to do it, free to do it some other way, to argue.

In the army the commanding officer may be objectionable. He may harass, discriminate, make senseless demands and, at a critical moment, disappear without having given any orders. And without an order nothing can be done.

Men talk about him, think and dream about him. Not so in civilian life: it's possible to argue, to apply persuasion, to quarrel, to threaten.

The effect is the same.

Boredom.

Boredom in the front lines is short-lived. Already someone is knocking at the door of the peasant hut, a horse has snorted along the road. There's news on the way. Maybe there'll be a move to town, maybe the next night will be spent in a palace, or moving to another front line, or maybe the worst is in store—captivity.

And now, here, we the Jews also don't know what tomorrow holds for us. And yet there's a sense of security. Thus, boredom.

Would you rather be in the battle of Kharkov?

I have brushed aside with scorn all the rubbish printed in the newspapers and I replied:
"I would."
It's worse, perhaps, but different, anyway.
This is why some escape by indulging in trade, others in black marketeering, in social work, in [. . .]
It's daylight again. I yawn. One more day.
That darned tooth that makes my tongue so sore—what a nuisance. I've filed it down, to no avail. Perhaps it's cancer, perhaps my time has come?

May 29, 1942, six in the morning in bed

If you want to check your resistance to madness try to help a shlemiel.
You put the paper right into her hand. She's to deliver it—tomorrow to someone personally—here is the address and the hour. But she's lost the paper or forgot to take it with her, or had no time, or the porter advised her to do something else. She will go tomorrow. It's all the same. Anyhow, she is not sure whether it will be all right. No one to leave the child with, she has some washing to do, just the child's dress.
"Couldn't you leave the washing till tomorrow?"
"It's hot. I promised."
She is upset. Perhaps nothing will come of it? Before the war such things were her husband's problem.
"Perhaps I'm no good, but please don't be angry with me."

I check on the financial situation of a family. They have applied for the admission of their boy.
"He can sleep here. It is quite clean."

"You call that clean? You should have seen our place before the war. . . ."

"He could be here with us all day."

"And if it rains?"

"It's not for me to decide. I have recorded my opinion, it is up to the ladies to say what is to be done."

"Doctor! You have no idea what a child he is! You'll see for yourself. You'll be sorry to have only one like him. I had five doctors with me at my confinement."

I do not say: "You're being silly."

I did say that once thirty years back to a mother in the hospital.

She answered: "If I were rich, I wouldn't be silly."

I say to another woman:

"Even Rothschild doesn't give his child more than five meals a day."

"His child will have enough to eat all his life."

I say:

"If your child needed to drink tea, God would have given you milk in one breast and tea in the other."

"If God would only give children what He can give, and what they need. . . ."

I say:

"If you don't believe me, you may call another doctor whom you trust."

"Please, doctor, I don't mean any offense, but how can I trust men if sometimes I don't trust even God?"

A woman says:

"When I had spanked his behind so hard that he seemed to be on fire, I was so sorry for him that, pardon my saying so, I began to cry."

Sami has just brought me a letter to bed: will this do?

"To the Reverend Father, The Vicar of All Saints:

"We kindly request the Rev. Father to grant us permission to come a few times to the church garden on Saturdays, in the morning hours, early if possible (6:30—10 a.m.).

"We long for a little air and greenery. It is stuffy and crowded where we are. We want to become acquainted and make friends with nature.

"We shall not damage the plants.

"Please don't refuse us.

> Zygmus
> Sami
> Abrasza
> Hanka
> Aronek."

How many treasures a man will lose when he no longer has the patience to talk to people with whom he has no business, merely for the sake of getting to know them better.

This application with which we began the day is today a good omen. Maybe I'll collect today more than fifty zlotys.

They sleep in the isolation room. Seven of them. Old Azrylewicz tops the list (*angina pectoris*), Genia (probably lung trouble), Haneczka (asthma). On the other side, Monius, Reginka, Maryla.

Hanka to Genia:

"He has sacrificed so much for her. He would have given his life for her and everything, everything in the world. And she didn't love him, the beast."

"Why beast? Must you love because he loves?"

"That depends how he loves. If he loves just a little, it doesn't matter, but if he is ready to give his life and everything, everything?"

"And did she ask him for anything?"

"Certainly not!"

"Well, you see."

"That's what I mean."

"No, you said she's a beast."

"Because she is."

"I don't want to talk any more."

They were angry at each other.

I feel content and discontent. I become angry, happy, anxious, indignant, I am eager to experience and to avoid experience, I am understanding but I call for punishment by God or man. I judge: this is good, this is bad.

But all this is theoretical. Made to order. Flat, drab, customary, professional; I perceive things as if through a fog, with blotched, non-dimensional emotions. They seem to be beside me, not inside me. I can quite easily give up, postpone, cancel, suspend, substitute.

The sharp tooth cuts into my tongue. I am witness to a revolting scene: I hear words that ought to shock me. I can't cough the phlegm up, my throat is blocked, I suffocate.

A shrug, it's all the same to me.

Indolence. Poverty of feeling, that eternal Jewish resignation: So what? And what next?

"What if my tongue is sore, what if some have been shot?" "He already knows he must die. And what next?" "Surely you cannot die more than once . . .?"

Occasionally, something will rouse me, and I am surprised, seem to realize or recollect that it is so, can be, was once. I see the same thing in others.

A chance meeting with someone we have not seen in many years. In his changed features, we read how different we ourselves have become from our previous lives, from what we were.

And in spite of all, from time to time. . . .

A following scene in the street:

A young boy, still alive or perhaps dead already is

55

lying across the sidewalk. Right there three boys are playing horses and drivers; their reins have gotten entangled. They try every which way to disentangle them, they grow impatient, stumble over the boy lying on the ground. Finally one of them says:

"Let's move on, he gets in the way."

They move a few steps away and continue to struggle with the reins.

Or: I check out an application for a boy to be admitted to the institution. 57 Smocza Street, apartment 57. Two decent families, dying out.

"I don't know if he will be willing to go to the institution right now. He's a good boy. Until his mother dies, too, he will be sorry to leave. The boy is out: he has gone scrounging for food."

The mother is lying on a couch:

"I can't die before he is settled somewhere. Such a good child: he tells me not to sleep in the daytime so as to be able to sleep at night. And at night he says: what are you moaning for, that won't help? You'd better go to sleep."

While the cabmen are quarrelsome, noisy and spiteful, the rickshaw men are gentle and quiet. Like horses or oxen.

On the corner of Solna and Leszno Streets, I notice a group of people consisting of an excited rickshaw man, an enraged peroxide blonde with crinkly hair, a policeman looking somewhat surprised, disappointed. Standing to one side, a smartly dressed woman looks on, evidently shocked. She waits to see how it will all end.

The policeman says gloomily:

"Better give the hooligan what he asks."

And he shuffles on.

The rickshaw man asks a rhetorical question:

"If the lady doesn't want to pay, then I'm a hooligan?"
She:

"I'll pay you two zlotys but you must take me to that house over there."

"You've agreed to three zlotys to the corner of Ciepla Street."

He turns around and rides away, parks in a line of rickshaws.

I asked the shocked elegant woman:

"Do you know what happened?"

"Yes, I was riding with her."

"Who was right?"

"He. But why does he give up two zlotys rather than take her that extra hundred feet?"

"He wants his own way."

"Evidently."

I go up to the rickshaw man.

"What was the trouble?"

"Nothing. I lost two zlotys. So what? I won't be any poorer, and I am a hooligan either way."

I related the incident to three sets of listeners,

I couldn't do otherwise. I simply had to.

One or two fellow workers from Dzielna Street, not without encouragement from a woman not from Dzielna Street, have denounced me to the Jewish Council or Chamber of Health for failing to report cases of typhoid fever. Failure to report even one case may carry a death sentence.

I went to the Health Office and managed to calm them down somewhat and fix things for the future. I wrote two letters to two offices. To one, that I promise and don't keep my promise. To the other I addressed a question: What do they plan to do with me and my new center at Dzielna Street?

The letters were not courteous. Not by any means. But can one justifiably call me a scoundrel?

Now I know: that woman's name is [. . .].

But if she is annoyed at me and a damn nuisance to the hospital system, and I wrote only that about her, then why am I a scoundrel?

What am I expected to do?

A small shopkeeper said to a customer with a complaint:

"My good woman—these are not goods and this is not a store, you are not a customer nor I a vendor, I don't sell to you nor do you pay me because these scraps of paper are not money. You don't lose, and I don't profit. Who would bother to cheat nowadays—for what? Only one's got to do something. Well, am I not right?"

If I were given a missal, I could in a pinch celebrate a mass.

But I should not be able to preach a sermon to the flock in armbands. I should swallow the sentences, read a question in their eyes:

"What now? And what next?"

The words would stick in my throat.

*

Sliska, Panska, Marianska, Komitetowa streets. Memories, memories, memories.

Every house, every courtyard. Here were my half-ruble calls, usually at night.

For medical advice in the daytime to the rich and in the rich streets, I asked three or five rubles. Brazen—as much as Anders, more than Kramsztyk, Baczkiewicz—professorial fees. I, a resident doctor, the general hack, the drudge at the Berson Hospital.

A thick volume of reminiscences.

58

Jewish doctors had no Christian clientele, only the well placed, living in well-to-do streets. And about these—proudly:

"I was called to the district police chief, the restaurant proprietor, the bank commissioner, the schoolmaster in the high school at Nowolipki Street, the postmaster."

That was already something.

And I had phone calls, not every day, of course:

"Countess Tarnowski would like to speak to you, Doctor. The Prosecutor General of the Judicial Chamber. Madam Tygajlo, wife of a big shot director. The lawyers Makowski, Szyszkowski."

I write down the address on any scrap of paper at hand, asking:

"Would it be all right tomorrow? After the hospital, say, at one. Is there a temperature? Yes, he may have a soft-boiled egg."

Even once:

"General Gilchenko's wife."

And by unimportant contrast: Captain Hopper, a phone call, sometimes two, each time the child had his bowel movement.

Such were the calls of the author of *Drawing-Room Child*,[15] while Goldszmit would go at night to the basement at 52 Sliska Street, to the attic at 17 Panska Street.

I was once called to the Poznanski residence[16] at Aleje Ujazdowskie.

It had to be today. The patients couldn't wait.

"Three rubles," said Dr. Julek, who knew everybody in Warsaw. "They're stingy."

So I went.

"Will you wait a moment, doctor? I'll send for the boys."

15. One of Korczak's early books.
16. Well-known family of textile manufacturers in Poland. (Trans.)

"Are they out?"

"Not far. They're playing in the park. Meanwhile—a cup of tea?"

"I can't spare the time to wait."

"But Doctor Julian always. . . . Have you been writing anything lately?"

"Unfortunately only prescriptions."

The next day:

"For God's sake, my friend!—They're furious. Enemies!"

"I don't give a damn."

"Well, well."

As resident doctor, I had accommodations and an annual salary of 200 rubles, paid quarterly. The house was kept by a good old soul to whom I paid fifteen rubles a month. From private practice I had a hundred rubles a month, and odd sums from articles, too.

I used to spend a lot on cabs.

"A cab to go to Zlota Street? Twenty kopecks? Spendthrift!"

I treated for free the children of socialists, teachers, newspaper men, young lawyers, even doctors—all progressive men.

Sometimes I phoned:

"I won't come till evening. I must bathe and change—we've quite a few cases of scarlet fever. I'd hate to infect the kid."

The kid!

This was the bright side.

And the shadows . . .

I declared:

"Since the older doctors don't want to be bothered at night, especially for the poor, I, being young, must hasten on these errands of mercy."

You understand. Immediate help. How else? What if the child does not last till morning?

Hospital attendants have declared war and they acquired drug wholesalers and two hostile pharmacies as allies.

The unanimous opinion—he is mad. A dangerous lunatic. They differed only in prognosis: is it curable?

Once, at night, a woman in a head scarf came to my door. It was pouring rain.

"My mother's ill."

"But I only treat children."

"She's gone all childish. I know you can't help so why do I bother? But the doctors don't want to write a death certificate. But she's my mother. And without a doctor?"

I went.

"I beg your pardon, I didn't know that you only treat children. Assistant Surgeon Blucharski sent me. A Jew, but a decent man. He said: 'My good woman, you'd have to pay me a ruble because it's a night call. But there's a doctor in the hospital—he'll come for nothing, and still leave some money for medicine'."

Out of spite, I had been signing prescriptions without the Dr.—doctor.

They would say:

"We don't know any doctor by that name, he's probably an orderly."

"But . . . a doctor in the hospital."

So:

"The medicine was prescribed by Dr. NK (not known, improper medicine)."[17]

I used to take twenty kopecks because "it is written in the Talmud that an unpaid doctor is no help to a sick man."

17. Father unknown.

For the most part I found the patients amusing. Funny people. Occasionally annoying.

The night bell. The ambulance brings a child suffering from burns.

"What do you think?"

"I don't. Nothing can be done."

"This is no ordinary child. I am a merchant. I have a house. I can pay."

"Please don't shout. Please leave, you'll wake the patients."

"What's that to me?"

The orderly and I took him under the arms, and out onto the stairs. The bed with the child in it was rolled into the surgery on the ground floor.

"You've got a telephone so you can summon as many Warsaw professors as you like!"

"I'll write to the papers about you. You'll be struck off the roll."

A night ruined.

Or: six o'clock in the morning. A woman enters my room.

"Come to see my child."

I'm still drowsy after a bad night.

"What's wrong with him?"

"Inflammation after scarlet fever."

"Who has been treating him?"

"Various people."

"Then you'd better call those various people."

"And what if I prefer you? I can pay."

"I don't go out at night."

"Is six in the morning night?"

"It's night."

"So you're not coming?"

"No."

Banging the door, she threw a final:

"An aristocrat! You just lost three rubles."

Without bargaining, she would have given me 25 kopecks, and three kopecks "for the janitor." She wanted to punish me: now he won't be able to sleep, chewing his fingers, furious with himself.

He's lost three rubles.

This is my native district Panska Street, Sliska Street.

I've abandoned the hospital for the Children's Home. I have a guilt complex.

Once I had to leave (because of the war).

The second time—a year in Berlin.

The third time—for less than six months, in Paris.

Toward enlightenment, toward knowledge.

Now that I know that I don't know and why I don't know, now that I can act in accordance with the supreme rule "don't harm the sick," I set out for unknown waters.

The hospital has given me a great deal, and I, ungrateful, have given it so little. An ugly desertion. Life has taken revenge.

Yesterday I went to Grzybow No. 1 to collect a donation. The last building before the ghetto wall. A Jewish policeman was killed here yesterday. They say he was signaling to smugglers.

"That's not the place for wholesale business," a neighbor explained.

The store is closed.

The people are scared.

Yesterday, in front of the house, the janitor's assistant:

"Doctor, you don't remember me?"

"Wait . . . of course, Szulc!"

"You do remember . . .?"

"Ah, I remember you too well. Come, tell me." We sat down on the church steps.

My goodness, Grzybow: here in 1905 Sobotka was wounded.

Two recollections intermingled. Bula is forty by now. Not long ago, he was ten.

"I have a child. Come and have some cabbage soup with us. You'll see him."

"I'm tired, I'm on my way home."

We talked for fifteen minutes, perhaps half an hour.

Shocked Catholics wearing armbands[18] stole discreet glances in our direction. They know me.

In broad daylight on the church doorstep Korczak is sitting with a smuggler. The children must need money badly. But why so openly, demonstratively, and, however you look at it, shamelessly?

It's a provocation. What would the Germans think if they saw this? Yes: the Jews are brazen and irritating.

And Szulc confides in me:

"In the morning, he has half a pint of milk, a roll and butter. That costs a pretty penny."

"What for?"

"He must know he's got a father."

"A rascal?"

"And why not. He's my son."

"And your wife?"

"A fine woman."

"Do you quarrel?"

"Been together for five years, never raised my voice at her once."

"And do you still remember?"

A suspicion of a smile.

"I think of the Children's Home often. Sometimes I dream about you and Madam Stefa."

"Why didn't you ever come during all these years?"

"When I was well off, I had no time. When I was down and out, how could I come—ragged and dirty?"

18. Catholics of Jewish descent.

64

"Do you ever see Lejbus?"

"No."

He helped me up. We kissed warmly, heartily.

He was too honest for a crook. And perhaps the Children's Home had sown some seed in him, and trimmed something down? All the time I believed that he had either gotten rich or was no more.

"My partner is rich."

"He helps you a bit?"

"Not he."

How quickly the hours pass. Just now it was midnight—and already it's three in the morning. I had a visitor in my bed.

Mendelek had a bad dream. I carried him to my bed. He stroked my face (!) and went to sleep.

He squeals. He's uncomfortable.

"Are you asleep?"

"I thought I was in the dormitory."

He stares surprised with his black monkeylike beads of eyes.

"You were in the dormitory. Do you want to go back to your own bed?"

"Am I in your way?"

"Lie down at the other end. I'll bring you the pillow."

"Fine."

"I'll be writing. If you're frightened, come back."

"O.K."

Also a grandson. The youngest Nadanowski.

Jakub has written some sort of poem about Moses. If I don't read it today, he may feel hurt.

With satisfaction and melancholy, I am reading his and Monius's diaries. Differing in age, and even more in intellect, in style of life—yet emotionally alike.

Men of broad expanse, of equal level.

There was a strong wind and dust yesterday. Passers-by squinted and covered their eyes.

I remember a scene observed during a sea voyage. A little girl stood on the deck. A sapphire sea in the background. There was a sudden gust of wind. She closed her eyes and covered them with her hands. However, curious, she looked up and—amazing!—the wind was clean, for the first time in her life. Nothing to get into their eyes. She tried it twice before she felt reassured, and she rested her elbows on the rail. And the wind caressed and combed her hair. Boldly she opened her eyes as wide as possible. Embarrassed, she smiled.

"There is such a thing as wind without dirty dust but I didn't know about it. I didn't know there was pure air anywhere in the world. And now I know."

A boy said to me when he left the Children's Home:

"Were it not for the home I wouldn't know that there are honest people in the world who never steal. I wouldn't know that one can speak the truth. I wouldn't know that there are just laws in the world."

The program for this Sunday.

In the morning, 39 Dzielna Street.[19] On the way, see Kohn.

I received a notice to pay a fine following the case I

19. Here the municipal orphanage was moved from Plocka Street and was taken over by the Jewish Council. This orphanage was turned into a kind of children's rescue station: sick, abandoned children were collected on the streets and brought there. The number of deaths gives an idea of the conditions and the situation: ten to fifteen deaths daily. The Doctor took upon himself to reform this "pre-funeral home," as he called it. The depraved personnel did everything possible to fight the new curator, and the council administration was not too cooperative either (when, for example, Korczak requested a twenty thousand zloty grant, they offered him one thousand). No wonder Korczak had to pay with his health for every day spent at this institution.

66

had. Five hundred zlotys a month. So, including today (June 1), I ought to pay fifteen hundred zlotys. Should I default, the whole amount, three or five thousand—I don't remember exactly—would be payable at once.

The point is that I want them to accept my savings book with 3000 zlotys. I suggested this when they asked me at Szuch Avenue[20] whether the Jewish community office would not pay bail for my release.

"Don't you want the community office to pay for you?"

"No."

It was then that they wrote down that I had 3000 zlotys in a savings book.

Several weeks, rich in developments, have gone by.

I stopped writing because Heniek was sick, and I thought there was nobody to type up my nightly revelations.

Curiously enough, I believed that to be true, although I knew that several other boys could do it equally well.

It would have been a different matter if I had decided to make writing a daily duty. As during the war. *How To Love a Child* was typed even during halts of a few hours. At Jeziorna, even Walenty rebelled.[21]

"Is it worthwhile for just half an hour?"

And then in Kiev, too, it was absolutely every day.

And now I am finishing my pad. Another excuse to write no more tonight, though I feel perfectly rested. I had four cups of strong coffee, prepared from dregs, it's true, but reinforced I suspect with fresh-ground coffee.

We do deceive ourselves: I have no more paper. I shall read Diderot's *Jacques le fataliste*.

---

20. Gestapo headquarters in Warsaw. (Trans.).

21. It appears that during World War I Korczak's orderly objected to his notes, which deprived him of rest.

Probably for the first time I have forgotten that I am living through my tenth seven-year life stage, 7×9.

Tensely, I waited for 2×7. Perhaps it was precisely then that I had heard of this for the first time.

The Gypsy's seven, seven days of the week. Why not the victorious ten of olden days (the number of fingers)?

I remember the tense feeling as I waited for the clock to strike midnight. The change was supposed to take place just at that instant.

There was some scandal with a hermaphrodite. I am not sure whether it was exactly at that time. I don't quite know whether I was afraid that I might wake up to find I was a girl. I made up my mind that if that happened I would keep it secret at all costs.

Gepner[22] 7×10, I—7×9. If I go over my life, the seventh year of age brought me a sense of my own value. I exist. I have·weight. I have meaning. I am visible. I can. I will.

Fourteen. I look around. I perceive. I see. . . . My eyes were due to open. They did. My first ideas concerning education reforms. I read a lot. My first anxieties and frustrations. Now, imagined voyages and stormy adventures, then again a quiet family life, friendship (love) for Stach. The primary dream among many, among many dozens: he's a priest, I a doctor in that small town. I thought of love, formerly I only felt it, I loved. From seven to fourteen I was permanently in love, always with a different girl. Odd, but I remember many of them. The two sisters from the skating rink, Stach's cousin (her grandfather was Italian), the one in mourning, Zosia Kalhorn, Anielka, Irenka from Naleczow. Stefcia for whom I used to pick flowers from the beds by the fountain in Saski Park. Then that little tightrope dancer, I

---

22. A well-to-do philanthropist supporting the Children's Home.

grieved bitterly over her fate. I loved for a week, a month, occasionally two at once, three. One I wanted to have for a sister, another for a wife, for a sister-in-law. . . . My love for Mania from my fourteenth year (at Wawer in summer) was an integral part of that [. . .] of feelings that alternately gently rocked or violently shook me. The exciting world was not already behind me. Now it is within me. I exist not to be loved and admired, but myself to act and love. It is not the duty of those around to help me but I am duty-bound to look after the world, after man.

3×7. In the seventh year, school, in the fourteenth, religious maturity, in the twenty-first, military service. For a long time I've had the feeling of being cooped up. Once I was imprisoned by the school. Now I am generally shut in. I want to prevail, fight for new areas.

(Probably these thoughts were suggested to me by the 22nd of June when, after the longest day of the year, the sun sets three minutes earlier each day. Sneakingly, imperceptibly but inexorably there is less of the day by three minutes and again by three, and again. I used to commiserate with old age and death; now, less sure myself, I begin to fear for my own self. One must fight for and achieve a great balance in order to have enough to write off for losses. Perhaps it was precisely then that the dentist pulled out my first adult tooth which would not grow again. My rebellion against the law of nature, not social conditions, came to a head. Get ready, aim, fire.)

4×7. The need for efficient functioning over the limited area of one's own "workshop." I am anxious to achieve, to know, not to idle, not to stray. I need to be a good doctor. I shape a model of my own. I do not wish to model myself upon acknowledged authorities. (Things used to be otherwise once. Even today there are moments when I feel like a young man with a long road

ahead. I find it worthwhile to plan and venture anew. In
the second, and certainly in the third seven years, I felt
so old at times, that everything was a constant repetition,
already too late, not worthwhile. Indeed, life is like a
flame. It dies down though there is ample fuel. Suddenly, when it is about to die down, it flares up, sending
out sparks and shooting up brightly. And it dies out. A
hot day in the fall and the awareness that this is the last,
exceptional, cold morning in July.)

5×7. I got my money back in the lottery of life. My
number is already drawn. My money back. So I will not
lose in this drawing unless I stake again. Might have
been worse: I might have lost. But no more chance of the
big prize—a pity. Fair enough—I have gotten back what
I paid in. Safe. But drab—and regrettable.

Loneliness does not hurt. I value memories. A
schoolmate—a friendly chat over a cup of coffee in a
quiet corner where no one will disturb us. I seek no
friend because I know I will not find one. I do not strive
to know more than it is possible. I have signed a pact
with life: we will not get in each other's way. It's unbe-
coming to fly at each other—no use anyway. In politics, I
believe, they call it a demarcation of the spheres of influence. So far and no more, no farther, no higher. You
and I.

6×7. Perhaps? Already, or not yet? That depends. Let
us balance the books. Assets, liabilities. If one knew how
many years were left, when the end would come. I do
not feel the inner call of death, but already I think about
it. When a tailor makes me a new suit, I do not say:
that'll be the last. But the office desk and the chest of
drawers will surely outlive me. There'll be no wild es-
capades, no surprises. There'll be more severe or milder
winters, rainy and scorching summers. And gratifying
coolness, and gales, and dust storms. So I will say: in ten,

fifteen years we have not had such hail, such floods. I remember a similar fire. I was young then, let me think—already a university student or still a schoolboy?

7×7. What is life really, what is happiness? So long as it is not worse, just as it is now. Two sevens have met and exchanged polite greetings, glad that things are as they are, and precisely here, and under such specific conditions. A newspaper—seemingly only mindless reading. Perhaps it is. Yet you cannot do without it. There are the editorials, and a novel in installments, obituaries and theatrical reviews, reports from the courts. The movies—a new film. A new novel. Small accidents. Classified advertisements. Not really so interesting as rather offering a choice. Someone killed under the streetcar, somebody has invented something or other, someone's fur coat was stolen, and here a five-year prison sentence. Somebody wants to buy a sewing machine or a typewriter, or has a piano for sale or is looking for a three-room apartment with all modern conveniences. A broad river bed, I should say, of the majestically flowing Vistula River as it flows near Warsaw.

My city, my street, the store where I regularly shop, my tailor, and most important of all—my workshop.

As long as it is no worse. For, if one could say to the sun: stop, probably it should be at this time of life. (There is a small dissertation *On the Happiest Period of Life*—and, believe it or not, by Karamzin.[23] His stuff sure bothered us in the Russian school.)

7×8 = 56. How these years have flown. Literally flown. It seems but yesterday that it was 7×7. Nothing added, nothing subtracted. What a vast difference in the ages: seven and fourteen, fourteen and twenty-one. And for me, at 7×7 and 7×8—absolutely the same.

23. N. N. Karamzin (1766–1826) Russian writer and historian.

Please do not get me wrong. Obviously there are no two identical leaves, nor drops, nor grains of sand. This fellow has a balder head, that one more gray hair. This one has false teeth, that one only caps. This one wears eyeglasses, that one is hard of hearing. This one is more bony, that one is fatter. But I am speaking of the seven-year stages.

I know: life could be divided into five-year periods, and that way, too, it could be made to fit. I know: the living conditions. Wealth, poverty. Success, worries. I know the war, wars, disasters. And this too is relative. A certain lady told me: "The war has spoiled me and later it was very difficult to settle down." Even the present war is spoiling many. Yet surely there is not a man who does not believe that the failures of strength, health and energy spring not from the war but from that 7×8 and 7×9.

What ghastly dreams! Last night: the Germans, I without an armband during a curfew at Praga.[24] I woke up. And again a dream. On a train, I am moved, a meter at a time, into a compartment where there are already several Jews. Again some had died tonight. Bodies of dead children. One dead child in a bucket. Another skinned, lying on the boards in the mortuary, clearly still breathing. Another dream: I am standing high up on a wobbly ladder, and my father keeps on pushing a piece of cake into my mouth, a big lump with sugar frosting and raisins, and anything that falls from my mouth he puts crumbed into his pocket.

I woke up in a sweat at the most crucial point. Is not death such an awakening at a point when there is no apparent way out?

"Every man can surely find five minutes in which to die"—I have read somewhere.

24. The section of Warsaw east of the Vistula.

72

Summer. 39 Dzielna Street. Abstracts.

When the tenth person in turn pesters me about a decision regarding the candy and the honeycakes—it drives me crazy. Are there no other problems to solve except those of the honeycakes!

Yesterday, a little boy came back from the hospital after having had a leg amputated following frostbite. Everybody thinks it his duty to tell me about it. What annoying thoughtlessness! I'll put up with it. But that boy—a hero of the day?

Too few hysterics around here, it seems.

*

Two sensible, level-headed, unbiased informants and advisers have let me down. The weighing machine and the thermometer.

I have ceased to believe them. They too tell lies.

*

We say:

Group one, group two—area A, area B, area C. We say: the wing. (The wing has not had its breakfast yet.) We say: area U, area I. Group A of boys and girls alternately . . .

Is it incidental, some sort of historical rudiments, or a desire to intimidate and flabbergast a newcomer?

Hard to say.

*

We have various kinds of "men": a barrow man, an errand boy, a porter or janitor. We have women workers, house servants, charwomen, governesses—today a hygienist has emerged. We have section managers, floor or landing stewards, probably keyguards as well. Such things did not bother me in jail, but here it is upsetting.

All this is difficult to grasp.

*

There are women for the morning, the afternoon, the night, ill, convalescent, feverish, temporary, group leaders, half-and-halves, outside workers, the dismissed.

Hard to say who's who.

*

She looks at me with alarm in her eyes and answers: I don't know.

As if she came yesterday, hasn't worked here for ten years but only came yesterday. As if what I am asking related to the North Pole or the equator.

She doesn't know. Just does her job.

The only way: not to interfere and not to know what the hundred-headed roll of employees do.

*

Children?

Not only children but cattle, and carrion, and dung.

I have caught myself in a transgression. I do not give them a full teaspoon of cod liver oil. I think that on their graves will grow nettle, burdock and madwort, not nutritious vegetables and flowers, oh no.

*

I have the impression that they send us here the mere

74

leavings of children and of staff from allied institutions. An imbecile, a spiteful predator expelled from the Children's Home, has landed here, too. When finally a German soldier intervened in his behalf, I told the policeman that if Fula were to come back I would take his gun and stand guard, and let him, the policeman, take charge of the Home.

So the mother placed him here.

*

The staff.
A chimney sweep must be smeared with soot.
A butcher must be stained with blood (a surgeon, too).
A cesspool cleaner stinks.
A waiter must be crafty. If he is not, woe be unto him.
I feel all smeared, blood-stained, stinking. And crafty, since I am alive—I sleep, eat and, occasionally I even joke.

*

I have invited for consultation:
Brokman
Mrs. Heller
Przedborski
Gantz-Kohn
Lifszyc
Mayzner
Mrs. Zand[25]
Now advise me: limewater: all right. What else?

*

25. An attorney and several physicians working in the ghetto.

Long after the war, men will not be able to look each other in the eyes without reading the question: How did it happen that you survived? How did you do it?

My dear Anka. . . .

1. I don't make social calls. I go to beg for money, foodstuffs, an item of information, a lead. If you call that social calls . . . they are arduous, degrading work. Must play the clown, too. People don't like gloomy faces.

I often call on the Chmielarz family. They always find some food for me. That's not a social call, either. I see it as a good deed, they—as an exchange of services. In spite of the kind, gentle and soothing atmosphere, it is frequently tiring, too.

Reading as relaxation begins to fail. A dangerous symptom. I am distracted and that itself worries me. I don't want to sink into idiocy.

2. I have sent the 500 zlotys. If I am in any danger, the least from that side, in that case. A reliable and stalwart friend—an excellent lawyer—looks after the matter. I take no steps without his approval.

3. I am going to see the head of the Staff Section. I could not have failed to consider the case since there was none. Whatever Madam Stefa said, promised and undertook, I did not know since no one told me. I have kept the secret.

4. In my humble opinion, I discharge my duties to the best of my ability. I never refuse if I can help it. I have never undertaken to look after cops, so that charge is unjust.

June 26, 1942.

END OF PART ONE

I have read it over. I could hardly understand it. And the reader?

No wonder, that the memoirs are incomprehensible to the reader. Is it possible to understand someone else's reminiscences, someone else's life?

It seems that I ought to be able to perceive without effort what I myself write about.

Ah, but is it possible to understand one's own remembrances?

*

Slowacki left behind his letters to his mother. They give a vivid picture of his experiences over several years. Because of these letters, a document has survived attesting to his transformation under the influence of Towianski.[26]

It has crossed my mind:

"Perhaps I should write these diaries in the form of letters to my sister?"

Cold, strange, detached was my first letter to her. A reply to her letter.

And here:

"My dear . . ."

. . . .

What a great and painful misunderstanding.

*

Proust is sprawling and overly detailed?
Far from it!

26. Founder of a religious sect among Polish emigrants in France in XIX century. His ideas of Messianism had a great influence on Polish poets and writers of that time.

Every hour—a heavy volume, an hour's reading.
So be it.
You have to read all day to understand a day of mine,
more or less. Week after week, year after year.
And we, during a few hours, just a few hours of our
time, want to relive a whole lifetime.
No way. You may grasp some vague summary in a
careless sketch—a single episode in a thousand, in a
hundred thousand.

I am writing this in the classroom during a Hebrew
lesson.
Zamenhof[27] comes to my mind. Naive, audacious: he
wanted to rectify God's error or God's punishment. He
wanted to fuse the misplaced languages into one again.
Stop!
We must divide, divide, divide. Not fuse.
What would man have?
We must fill his time, give him something to do, a goal
in life.
"He speaks three languages. He is studying a language. He knows five languages."
Here we have two groups of children who have given
up amusement, easy books, chats with friends for a vol-
untary study of Hebrew.
When the younger group finished their hour, one stu-
dent exclaimed with surprise:
"What, an hour has passed already?"
So. "Da" in Russian, "ja" in German, "oui" in French,
"yes" in English, "ken" in Hebrew. Enough to fill not
one but three lives.

27. Warsaw physician, the inventor of Esperanto (1859–1917).

PART TWO

Today is Monday. From eight to nine a pupil's hostel chat. Whoever wants to may attend. Provided he does not interrupt.

Suggested themes:
1. The emancipation of women
2. Heredity
3. Loneliness
4. Napoleon
5. What is duty?
6. On the medical profession
7. Amiel's memoirs[1]
8. From the doctor's reminiscences
9. On London
10. On Mendel
11. Leonardo da Vinci
12. On Fabre
13. The senses and the mind
14. The genius and his surroundings (mutual impact)
15. The Encyclopedists
16. How different writers worked
17. Nationality. Nation. Cosmopolitanism
18. Symbiosis
19. Evil and malice
20. Freedom. Destiny and free will.

When I was the editor of "Maly Przeglad,"[2] only two themes attracted young people:

Communism (politics) and sexual problems.

1. French poet who became known when his memoirs were posthumously published (1821–1881).
2. A weekly supplement to the prewar Warsaw daily "Nasz Przeglad."

Wicked, shameful years—destructive, base. Prewar years, lying, hypocritical. Cursed years.

Life was not worth living.

Filth. Stinking filth.

Then the storm came. Cleared the air. Made breathing easier. More oxygen.

*

I devote this tale
to Szymonek Jakubowicz

From the series:
"STRANGE HAPPENINGS"

Let the planet be called Ro, and he be named Professor, Astronomer or whatever you like. And we shall call the place on Planet Ro where Professor Zi was making his observations a laboratory.

The name of the instrument in our imperfect speech will be a bit too long: "astropsychomicrometer," a micrometer in the medium of astral psychical vibrations.

In terms of our terrestrial observatories, the Professor used a telescope which, by buzzing, communicated what was going on here and there in the universe, and possibly the intricate instrument projected pictures onto a screen or recorded vibrations in the same way as a seismograph.

Anyhow, this is unimportant.

What is important is that the scientist from Planet Ro could control psychic energy and could change heat radiation into spiritual, or to be more precise, moral power.

All right. So long as we take morality to be the harmony of impressions and the equilibrium of feelings.

One more comparison comes to mind: a radio that

82

transmits not songs and music or war communiqués but rays of spiritual order. In the life of stars, and not merely in our own solar system.

Order and tranquillity.

And so Professor Zi sits troubled in his workroom and thinks:

"That restless spark which is Earth is again in ferment. Disorder, disquiet, negative emotions predominate, reign. Miserable, painful, impure is their life over there. Its disorders upset the current of time and of impressions. . . .

"The pointer has wavered again. The line of suffering has gone up violently."

One, two, three, four, five.

Astronomer Zi frowns.

"Should one put an end to this senseless game? This bloody game? The beings inhabiting the earth have blood. And tears. And they moan when hurt. Don't they want to be happy? Are they wandering, unable to find the way? It is dark down there, a gale and a dust storm blinds them."

The pointer quickly records more and more turbulence.

Improperly used steel administers penalty. But at the same time it guides and educates, prepares the proper spirit for new conquests and initiations.

"There are bodies of water upon that distant speck of light. From slaughtered trees you have built floating houses, braced them with steel. What a stupendous effort! You're unruly, indolent, but capable. You have no wings yet. How vast the flying heights and the expanse of oceans must seem to you."

Bzzzz . . . Bzzzz. . . .

"And instead of rejoicing in their hearts, in song with

an intensified collective effort, instead of tying the threads together, they tangle them and tear.

"What am I to do then? To check them would mean to force them onto a road for which they are not yet sufficiently mature, an effort beyond their strength and a goal transcending their present comprehension. No doubt they themselves are doing the same. Slavery, coercion, violence. Things which disturb, provoke and hurt."

Professor Zi sighs. Closes his eyes. Applies the sensor of the astropsychomicrometer to his chest and listens.

And there is a war on earth. Fires, smoldering ruins, battlefields. Man, responsible for the Earth and its products, does not know, or knows but understands for himself alone.

The space over Planet Ro (perhaps Lo) is filled with the blue, with the fragrance of the lily of the valley and the sweetness of wine. Winged feelings flicker like snowflakes, raising a song after a song, gentle and pure.

Our earth is still young. And a beginning is painful labor.

*

From the diaries they bring over for reading.

Marceli writes:

"I have found a penknife. I will give 15 groszy to the poor. I have promised myself."

Szlama:

"A widow sits at home and weeps. Perhaps the older son will bring something from his smuggling. She does not know that a gendarme has shot her son dead. . . . But do you know that soon everything will be all right again?"

Szymonek:

"My father was a fighter for a piece of bread. Although father was busy all day, yet he loved me."

(And two shocking memories.)

Natek: "Chess was invented by a Persian wizard or king."

Mietek: "That siddur[3] which I want to have bound is a souvenir since it belonged to my brother who died, and it was sent to him for the day of his bar mitzvah by his brother in Palestine."

Leon: "I needed a box to keep all sorts of souvenirs. Hersz wanted to sell me a French polished box for 3½ zlotys." (Here follows an involved account of the deal.)

Szmulek: "I have bought little nails for 20 groszy. Tomorrow I will have big expenses."

Abus: "If I sit a bit longer in the toilet, right away they say that I am selfish. And I want to be liked by others." (I know this problem from jail.)

I have fixed a toilet-fee scale:

1. For number one—catch five flies.
2. For number two—second class (a bucket-stool-with-a-hole combination)—ten flies.
3. First class—a toilet seat—fifteen flies.

One of the boys asks:

"May I pay the flies later? I can't wait."

Another:

"You go and do it, go on. . . . I'll catch them for you."

Every fly caught in the isolation room counts as two.

"And does it count if a fly is hit and gets away?" When you've got it, you've got it, there are certainly very few flies. Using the same system, a dozen or so years ago, kindergarten children caught all the bedbugs at Goclawek.

Community good will—what a mighty force.

3. Prayer book.

EUTHANASIA

The church has shrouded in ritual the functions of birth, marriage and death.

The ritual of the mass has taken possession of man's entire spiritual life, controlling even the accessory economic life of the flock.

When men cast away (why so abruptly?) the childish cloth, already tight and too short—artless and repeatedly patched up—the flock—the church expanded into a number of institutions.

Now construction is not only in the service of places of worship. The first, to be sure, was France, Paris who erected the contemporary tower of Babel. Its name is the Eiffel Tower.

There is the building of schools and secular universities, theaters, museums, concert halls, crematoria, hotels, stadiums—huge, magnificent, hygienic, modern.

There are now speeches over the radio, not only a sermon and the priest's address.

There are libraries, printing shops, bookstores, not only a holy book or a scroll on the altar and a street stand with holy objects.

There is the physician—the mighty structure of medicine. Now it is no longer the priest's prayer which protects against disease.

Against hail, and flood, fire and pestilence—there is now health care and insurance companies.

Social welfare replaces the one-time penny for the blind.

Sculpture and paintings on canvas are in art galleries, not only on ceilings and walls of houses of worship.

There are meteorological institutes instead of prayer services.

The hospital has grown out of the church.

All was contained within it and took its beginnings from it.

Now the stock exchange, not the square in front of the church, controls prices.

There are international meetings of learned specialists and countless periodicals, in place of the exchange of private letters and mutual social calls, discussions and feasts of the Levites.

Diplomacy, no less effective than prayers, protects us against the outbreak of war.

The penal, civil, and commercial codes are the equivalent of the old decalogue and its commentaries.

Prisons are former cloisters. Court verdicts—excommunications.

The man of today has matured, but he has not become wiser and gentler.

Once upon a time, everything was within the church, whatever was lofty, solemn, rational, beautiful, humanitarian, humane. Nothing was outside it but the beast of burden, numbed, exploited, helpless.

And even today, even at the very peak of development and knowledge, men have founded their most important affairs upon baptism, the sacraments of marriage, and rites linked with the hour of death for some and inheritance for the survivors.

So very recently, yes, almost yesterday, there appeared at the conference tables: the subject of population and birth control, the discussion on the perfect marriage and—euthanasia.

The right to kill as an act of mercy belongs to him who loves, and suffers—if he himself also does not want to remain alive. It will be this way in a few years.

An odd saying has come into use:

"To be a sociable, a Gypsy has gone to the gallows."

87

When on my sister's return from Paris I suggested to her that we should commit suicide together, there was no idea or program of bankruptcy involved. On the contrary. I could find no place for myself in the world or in life.

Qui bono that dozen odd years more? Perhaps it was my fault, who knows, that I did not repeat my offer. The deal did not materialize because of the differences of opinion.

When during the dark hours I pondered over the killing (putting to sleep) of infants and old people of the Jewish ghetto, I saw it as a murder of the sick and feeble, as an assassination of the innocents.

A nurse from the cancer ward told me that she used to put a lethal dose of medicine by the bedside of her patients, instructing them:

"Not more than one spoonful, because it's poison. One spoonful will alleviate the pain like medicine."

And over many years, not a single patient has reached for the fatal dose.

How will this problem look in the future?

An official board, what else? A well-developed organization. One big office, small rooms. Office desks. Lawyers, doctors, philosophers, business advisers, of different ages and specialties.

A person submits an application. Everybody is eligible. There are, perhaps, ample restrictions so that applications would not be made without proper consideration or not in earnest, deceitfully taking advantage of the board or to trick one's own family.

An application for death might serve to exert pressure upon the family:

"Come back to me, dear wife, or else—here's a receipt for my death application. . . . Daddy, I need money to have a good time.

"If you don't give me a passing grade in my matricula-
tion, you will suffer pangs of conscience, I'll poison your
peace of mind."

So:

The application must be on a specified kind of paper
only. Say, in Greek or Latin. A list of witnesses is necessary. Perhaps stamps. Perhaps a fee payable in four quarterly installments or three monthly, or seven weekly
installments.

The application must be well substantiated.

"I do not want to live because of a disease, a financial
crash, a disappointment, a surfeit, because my father,
son, friend has failed me.

"I request that the operation be performed within one
week, without delay."

Has anyone ever collected incidents and experiences,
confidences, letters, memoirs from concentration camps,
prisons, from condemned men or those threatened with
a death sentence, on the eve of a big battle, on the stock
exchange, in gambling houses?

The application is accepted. The formalities complied
with. Now comes an examination, conducted along the
same lines as a trial in court.

A medical examination. A consultation with a psychologist. Perhaps a confession, maybe psychoanalysis.

Additional interviews with witnesses.

Fixing the dates, any possible changes.

The specialists and the experts.

There may be a postponment of the implementation of
a favorable decision. Or a trial euthanasia. For it happens
that a man, having once tried the delights and joys of
committing suicide, lives to an advanced age never trying again.

One of the initiation processes for freemasons is said to

be such a test consisting of an unsuccessful leap into the unknown.

The place of execution. This is my personal invention—after a cut-off date.

Or:

"Proceed to this or that place. There you will receive the death you applied for. Your request will be granted in ten days' time at a morning, evening hour.

The authorities are requested to assist on land, at sea and in the air."

It looks as if I am joking. But no.

There are problems that lie, like bloodstained rags, right across the sidewalk. People cross to the other side of the street or turn their eyes away in order not to see.

I do the same.

However, where a broad issue and not just one beggar dying of starvation, is involved, this is not allowed. At stake is not merely one or a hundred miserable wretches in a hard year of war but millions through the centuries.

This you must look straight in the face.

My life has been difficult but interesting. In my younger days I asked God for precisely that.

"God, give me a hard life but let it be beautiful, rich and aspiring."

On discovering that Slowacki had done the same, I felt rather pained that it was not my invention, that I had a precursor.

When I was seventeen, I even started writing a novel entitled *Suicide*. The main character hated life out of fear of insanity.

I used to be desperately afraid of the lunatic asylum. My father was sent there several times.

So I am the son of a madman. A hereditary affliction.

90

More than two score years have gone by, and to this day this thought is at times a torment to me.

I am too fond of my follies not to be afraid that someone may try to treat me against my will.

At this point, I should say: part two. No. I have merely been longwinded. But I don't know how to be more concise.

July 15, 1942

A week's break in writing which, it seems, was absolutely necessary. I had the same feeling when writing *How To Love A Child*. I used to write at stops, in a meadow under a pine tree, sitting on a stump. Everything seemed important and if I did not note it down I would forget. An irretrievable loss to humanity. At times there was a pause for a month. Why make a fool of myself? That which is wise is known to a hundred men. When the proper time comes, they will tell you and act upon whatever is of major importance. It was not Edison who made the inventions; they were hanging as if on a line, like wash drying in the sun. All he did was to gather them off the line.

The same goes for Pasteur, the same for Pestalozzi. It is there. Only it must be expressed.

So it is with every problem.

If not one, then another, will launch himself first into space.

For a long time I could not understand in what way the present-day orphanage differs from the earlier ones, from our own as it once was.

The orphanage—barracks. I know.

The orphanage—prison. Yes.

The orphanage—beehive, anthill. No.

The Children's Home is now a home for the aged. I have seven occupants in the isolation room, three of whom are newcomers. The age of the patients ranges from seven right up to Azryl, sixty, who moans sitting on his bed with his legs dangling, and elbows resting on the back of a chair.

The morning discussions of the children are the result of temperature taking. What's my temperature, and what's yours? Who's feeling worse? How did they pass the night?

A sanatorium for rich patients, capricious, affectionately attached to their ailments.

Leon has fainted for the first time in his life. Now he is trying to find the cause.

The children moon about. Only the outer appearances are normal. Underneath lurks weariness, discouragement, anger, mutiny, mistrust, resentment, longing.

The seriousness of their diaries hurts. In response to their confidences I share mine with them as an equal. Our common experiences—theirs and mine. Mine are more diluted, watered down, otherwise the same.

*

Yesterday, while counting the votes of the staff at Dzielna Street, I understood the essence of their solidarity.

They hate one another but none of them will allow the other to come to harm.

"Don't meddle in our affairs. You are a stranger, an enemy. Even if you offer something useful it is only an illusion and will ultimately do harm."

The most devoted nurse, Miss Wittlin, had died—tuberculosis.

Too bad—Wittlin. Two: school and the isolation room.

"The salt of the earth" dissolves—the manure remains.
What will be the upshot?
"It is harder to live a day right than to write a book."
Every day, not just yesterday, is a book—a thick volume, a chapter, enough for many years.
How improbably long a man is alive.
There's nothing absurd about the calculations of the Holy Scriptures: Methuselah really did live about a thousand years.

Night, July 18

During the first week of our last stay at the Goclawek summer home, the result of the consumption of bread of unknown composition and make was a mass poisoning which affected the children and some of the staff.

Diarrhea. The excrements boiled over in the chamber pots. Bubbles formed upon the surface of the pitchlike matter. Bursting they exuded a sweetish-putrid odor, which not only attacked the sense of smell but invaded the throat, eyes, ears, the brain.

Just now we have something similar, but it consists of vomiting and watery stools.

During the night, the boys lost 80 kg among them—on the average a kilogram per head. The girls—60 kg (somewhat less).

The children's digestive tracts worked under heavy strain. Not much was needed to precipitate a disaster. Perhaps it was the inoculation against dysentery (five days ago) or the ground pepper added pursuant to a French recipe to the stale eggs used for Friday's *pâté*.

The next day, not so much as a single kilogram of the losses in weight was made up.

Help for those vomiting, moaning with pain, was administered in near darkness—with limewater. (Unlimited dental chalk for whoever wanted it, jug after jug. In addition, a drug for those suffering from headaches.) Finally, for the staff, sparingly—morphine. An injection of caffein for a hysterical new inmate following a collapse.

His mother, wasting away of ulcerated intestines, was unwilling to die until the child had been placed in the Home. The boy was unwilling to go until the mother had died. He finally yielded. The mother died propitiously, now the child has pangs of conscience. In his illness, he mimics his mother: he moans (screams), complains of pain, then gasps, then feels hot, finally is dying of thirst.

"Water!"

I pace the dormitory to and fro. Will there be an outbreak of mass hysteria? Might be!

But the children's confidence in the leadership prevailed. They believed that as long as the doctor was calm there was no danger.

Actually I was not so calm. But the fact that I shouted at the troublesome patient and threatened to throw him out onto the staircase was evidence that the man at the helm had everything under control. The decisive factor: he shouts, so he knows.

The next day, that was yesterday—the play. *The Post Office* by Tagore. Applause, handshakes, smiles, efforts at cordial conversation. (The chairwoman looked over the house after the performance and pronounced that though we are cramped, that genius Korczak had demonstrated that he could work miracles even in a rat hole.)

This is why others have been allotted palaces.

(This reminded me of the pompous opening ceremony of a new kindergarten in the workers' house at Gorczewska Street with the participation of Mrs. Moscicka[4]—the other one.)

4. Wife of the prewar President of Poland.

How ridiculous they are.

What would have happened if the actors of yesterday were to continue in their roles today?

Jerzyk fancied himself a fakir.

Chaimek—a real doctor.

Adek—the lord mayor.

(Perhaps illusions would be a good subject for the Wednesday dormitory talk. Illusions, their role in the life of mankind. . . .)

And so to Dzielna Street.

*

The same day. Midnight

If I were to say that I have never written a single line unwillingly, that would be the truth. But it would also be true to say that I have written everything under compulsion.

I was a child "able to play for hours on his own," and with me "you wouldn't know there was a child in the house."

I received building blocks (bricks) when I was six. I stopped playing with them when I was fourteen.

"Aren't you ashamed of yourself? Such a big guy. You ought to be doing something else. Reading. But blocks—what next. . . ."

When I was fifteen I acquired the craze, the frenzy of reading. The world vanished, only the book existed. . . .

I talked to people a lot: to peers and to much older grownups. In Saski Park I had some really aged friends. They "admired" me. A philosopher, they said.

I conversed only with myself.

For to talk and to converse are not the same. To change one's clothes and to undress are two different things.

I undress when alone, and I converse when alone.

A quarter of an hour ago I finished my monologue in the presence of Heniek Azrylewicz. Probably for the first time in my life I told myself positively:

"I have an analytical, not an inventive, mind."

To analyze in order to know?

No.

To analyze in order to find, to get to the bottom of things?

Not that either.

Rather to analyze in order to ask further and further questions.

I ask questions of men (of infants, of the aged), I question facts, events, fates. I am not so pressed for answers, I go on to other questions—not necessarily on the same subject.

My mother used to say:

"That boy has no ambition. It's all the same to him what he wears, whether he plays with children of his own kind or with the janitor's. He is not ashamed to play with toddlers."

I used to ask my building blocks, children, grownups, what they were. I did not break toys, it did not interest me why the doll's eyes closed when it was put down. It was not the mechanism but the essence of a thing, the thing for itself, in itself.

Writing a diary or a life story I am obliged to talk, not to converse.

Now back to euthanasia.

The family of a suicide.

Euthanasia to order.

An insane man, legally incapacitated, incapable of independent decision.

A code comprising a thousand articles is needed. Life itself will dictate them. What is important is the principle: it is permissible, desirable.

On a beautiful remote island, serene, as in a fairy tale, in a fine hotel, boarding house, a suicide casts the die. Is living worthwhile?

How many days or weeks are necessary to decide? A life following the patterns of contemporary magnates? Perhaps work?

The hotel service. Duties in shifts. The work in the garden. The length of stay?

"Where is he?"

"He has left."

To a neighboring island or to the bottom of the sea. Should there be a rule:

"The death sentence will be carried out in one month, even against your will. For you have signed an agreement, a contract with an organization, a deal with temporal life. So much the worse for you if you recant too late."

Or the death—liberation comes in sleep, in a glass of wine, while dancing, to the accompaniment of music, sudden and unexpected.

"I want to die because I'm in love."

"I long for death because I hate."

"Take my life because I am capable of neither love nor hate."

All this exists, but in crazy confusion, festering, filthy.

Death for profit, for a fixed payment, for convenience, to oblige.

Most intimately connected with death are sterilization, and the prevention and interruption of pregnancy.

"In Warsaw, you are free to have one child; in a small

97

town, two; in a village, three; in a frontier village, four. In Siberia, ten. Take your choice."

"Free to live but childless."

"Free to live but unmarried."

"Manage by yourself, pay the taxes exclusively for yourself."

"Here is a mate for you. Pick one out of ten, out of a hundred girls."

"You may have two males. We allow three females."

Hurrah! lots of jobs, files, agencies, offices!

(An iron machine does the work, provides accommodations, furniture, food, clothing. You are concerned only with organizing.)

A new method of land cultivation or livestock breeding, or new synthetic products, or the colonization of regions today inaccessible—the equator and the North and South Pole. The total population of the earth can be increased to five billion.

Communication has been established with a new planet. There is colonization. Mars, perhaps the moon will accept new immigrants. Perhaps there will be even more efficient means of communication with a distant neighbor. The result: ten billion men like you and me.

The earth has the last word as to who, where to, how many.

Today's war is a naive, though insincere, shoot-off. What is important is the great migration of peoples.

Russia's program is to mix and crossbreed. Germany's is to gather together those having a similar color of skin, hair, shape of nose, dimensions of the skull or pelvis.

Today, specialists feel the stranglehold of unemployment. There is a tragic quest for a *dish* of work for physicians and dentists.

Not enough tonsils waiting to be cut, appendixes to be taken out, teeth for filling.

"What to do? What to do?"

There is: *acetonemia, pylorospasmus*. There is: *angina pectoris*.

What will happen if we find that tuberculosis is not only curable but cured with a single injection, intravenal, intramuscular or subcutaneous?

Syphilis—test 606. Consumption, 2500. What will be left for doctors and nurses to do?

What will happen if alcohol is replaced by a whiff of gas? Machine No. 3. Price, ten zlotys. A fifty-year guarantee. The dose as prescribed on the label. Payable in installments.

If sufficient daily nourishment were contained in two *x*-bion pills, what about the chefs and the restaurants?

Esperanto? One daily newspaper for all peoples and all tongues. What will the linguists do, and above all, the translators and the teachers of foreign languages?

The radio—perfected. Even the most sensitive ear will detect no difference between live music and a "canned, conserved" melody.

What's going to happen when even today we need disasters to provide work and goals for just one generation?

We cannot go on like this, my dear friends. Because unprecedented stagnation will set in, and foul air such as no one has ever encountered, and frustration such as no one has ever experienced.

A theme for a short story.

Tomorrow begins a radio contest for the master violinist of the year, playing this or that symphony or dissonance.

The whole world is at the loudspeakers.

An unprecedented Olympic contest.

The fans of the violinist from the Isle of Parrots experience moments of terrible suspense.

Comes the final night.

Their favorite man is beaten.

They commit suicide, unable to reconcile themselves to the fall of their idol.

There is a Chekhov story: A ten-year-old nanny is so desperate for sleep that she strangles the screaming baby.

Poor nanny—she did not know what else to do. I have found a way. I don't hear the irritating coughing, I heartlessly ignore the aggressive and provoking behavior of the old tailor.

I don't hear it. Two o'clock in the morning. Silence. I settle down to sleep—for five hours. The rest I shall make up in the daytime.

I would like to tidy up what I have written. A tough assignment.

July 21, 1942

Tomorrow I shall be sixty-three or sixty-four years old. For some years, my father failed to obtain my birth certificate. I suffered a few difficult moments over that. Mother called it gross negligence: being a lawyer, father should not have delayed in the matter of the birth certificate.

I was named after my grandfather, his name was Hersh (Hirsh). Father had every right to call me Henryk: he himself was given the name Jozef. And to the rest of his children grandfather had given Christian names, too: Maria, Magdalena, Ludwik, Jakub, Karol. Yet he hesitated and procrastinated.

I ought to say a good deal about my father: I pursue in life that which he strove for and for which my grandfather tortured himself for many years.

100

And my mother. Later about that. I am both mother and father. That helps me to know and understand a great deal.

My great-grandfather was a glazier. I am glad: glass gives warmth and light.

It is a difficult thing to be born and to learn to live. Ahead of me is a much easier task: to die. After death, it may be difficult again, but I am not bothering about that. The last year, month or hour.

I should like to die consciously, in possession of my faculties. I don't know what I should say to the children by way of farewell. I should want to make clear to them only this—that the road is theirs to choose, freely.

Ten o'clock. Shots: two, several, two, one, several. Perhaps it is my own badly blacked out window.

But I do not stop writing.

On the contrary: it sharpens (a single shot) the thought.

July 22, 1942

Everything else has its limits, only brazen shamelessness is limitless.

The authorities have ordered the hospital in Stawki Street to be cleared. And the head doctor, a woman, was told to admit all the bad cases to Zelazna Street.

What do we do? Prompt decision, efficient action.

X and Z have 175 convalescent children. They have decided to place a third of them with me. There are more than fifteen other institutions, but ours is nearby.

And the fact that over a period of six months the lady in question stooped to every conceivable outrage against the patients for the sake of convenience, through obstinacy or stupidity, that she fought with devilish cunning against my humane and simple plan—that goes for nothing [. . .]

While I was out, Mrs. K. agreed to, and Mrs. S. proceeded to put in operation the shameless demand, detrimental in the highest degree, harmful to their children and ours [. . .].

To spit on the floor and clear out. I have long been contemplating it. More—a noose, or lead on the feet.

(It has come out incomprehensibly again. But I am too tired to write more.)

Azrylewicz died this morning. Oh, how hard it is to live, how easy to die!

July 27, 1942. Yesterday's rainbow.

Yesterday's rainbow.

A marvelous big moon over the camp of the homeless pilgrims.

Why can't I calm this unfortunate, insane quarter.

Only one brief communiqué.

The authorities might have allowed it.

Or, at worst, refused it.

Such a lucid plan.

Declare yourself, make your choice. We do not offer a choice of easy roads. No playing bridge for the time being, no sunbathing, no delicious dinners paid for with the blood of the smugglers.

Choose: either get out, or work here on the spot.

If you stay, you must do whatever may be necessary for the resettlers.

The autumn is near. They will need clothes, footwear, underwear, tools.

Anyone trying to wiggle out of it will be caught, anyone wanting to buy himself out—we shall gladly take his jewelry, foreign currency, anything of value. When he has already surrendered all—and fast—then we shall ask him again:

"Here or out there? What have you decided?"

So long as there's no sunbathing on the beaches, no bridge and no pleasant nap after reading the newspaper.

You're a social worker? All right. You can even pretend it for a time and we shall pretend to believe you. In general, we believe as long as it is convenient and whatever is convenient. Excuse me: not convenient. Whatever is in the plan.

We are running a gigantic enterprise. Its name is war. We work in a planned, disciplined manner, methodically. Your petty interests, ambitions, sentiments, whims, claims, resentments, cravings do not concern us.

Of course—a mother, a husband, a child, an old woman, a family heirloom, a favorite dish—they are all very nice, pleasant, touching. But for the present, there are more important things. When there is time to spare, we shall return to such things, too.

Meanwhile, in order not to prolong the matter, things must get a bit rough and painful, and if I may put it that way, without particular precision, elegance or even scrupulousness. Just roughly cut for current expediency.

You yourself are longing to see all this over. So are we. Therefore, don't interfere.

Jews go East. No bargaining. It is no longer the question of a Jewish grandmother but of where you are needed most—your hands, your brain, your time, your life. Grandmother. This was necessary only to hook on to something, a key, a slogan.

You say you cannot go East—you will die there. So choose something else. You are on your own, you must take the risk. For clearly we, to keep up appearances, are obliged to bar the way, to threaten, prosecute and reluctantly to punish.

And you butt in, uninvited, with a fresh wad of bank notes. We have neither time nor desire for that sort of thing. We are not playing at war, we were told to wage it with the greatest possible expedition, efficiently, as honestly as possible.

The job is not clean, or pleasant, or sweet smelling. So for the present we must be indulgent to the workers we need.

One likes vodka, another women, a third likes to boss everyone around while yet another, by contrast, is meek and lacks self-confidence.

We know: they have their vices, shortcomings. But they reported in time while you were philosophizing, procrastinating. Sorry, but the train must run on schedule, according to a timetable prepared in advance.

Here are the railroad tracks.

The Italians, the French, the Roumanians, the Czechs, the Hungarians—this way. The Japanese, the Chinese, even the Solomon Islanders, even the cannibals—the other way. Farmers, highlanders, the middle class and the intelligentsia.

We are Germans. It is not a question of the trademark but of the cost, the destination of the products.

We are the steel roller, the plow, the sickle. So long as it bears fruit. And it will, provided you don't interfere, don't whine, get all upset, poison the air. We may feel sorry for you at times, but we must use the whip, the big stick or the pencil, because there must be order.

A poster.

"Whoever does this or that—will be shot."

"Whoever does not do this or that—we will shoot."

Someone seems to be asking for it. A suicide? Too bad.

Someone else is not afraid. Hail! A hero?

104

Let his name shine in letters of gold but—now, out of the way since there is no alternative.

A third is afraid—livid with fear, constantly runs to the toilet, dulls himself with tobacco, liquor, women, and obstinately wants his own way. What would you do with him?

The Jews have their merits. They have talent, and Moses, and Christ, and are hard working, and Heine, are an ancient race, and progress, and Spinoza, and yeast and pioneering and generous. All true. But besides the Jews, there are other people, and there are other issues.

The Jews are important, but later—you will understand some day. Yes, we know and remember. An important issue, but not the only one.

We do not blame. It was the same with the Poles and it is the same even now with Poland and Palestine, and Malta, and Martinique, and with the respectable proletarian, and the fair sex and the orphan, with militarism and capitalism. But not all at once. There must be some order of procedure, some priorities.

It's hard for you, it's not easy for us, either. The more so since there is no buffet handy where formerly one could escape from a wearisome discussion.

You must listen my friend, to History's program speech about the new chapter.

WHY DO I CLEAR THE TABLE?

I know that many are dissatisfied at my clearing the table after meals. Even the orderlies seem to dislike it. Surely they can manage. There are enough of them. If there were not, one or two always could be added. Then why the ostentation, the obstinacy, and even maybe I'm nasty enough to pretend to be diligent and so democratic.

Even worse, if anyone comes to see me on important business, I tell him to wait, saying:

"I am occupied now."

What an occupation: picking up soup bowls, spoons and plates.

But worse still is that I do it clumsily, get in the way while the second helping is being passed. I bump against those sitting tightly packed at the tables. Because of me he cannot lick clean his soup plate or the tureen. Someone may even lose his second helping. Several times something fell from the plates carried clumsily. If anyone else had done it, he would be told off and have a case against him. Because of this eccentricity some seem to feel guilty for letting me do it, others feel guilty because somehow they think they are even taking advantage of me.

How is that I myself do not understand or see how it is? How can anyone understand why I do it when right now I am writing that I know, see and understand that instead of being helpful I make a nuisance of myself?

Odd. I sense that everybody thinks I should not pick up the dishes, but nobody has ever asked why I do it. Nobody has approached me: Why do you do it? Why do you get in the way?

But here is my explanation:

When I collect the dishes myself, I can see the cracked plates, the bent spoons, the scratches on the bowls. I expedite the clearing of the tables and the side table used for the little shop, so that the orderlies can tidy up sooner. I can see how the careless diners throw about, partly in a quasi-aristocratic and partly in a churlish manner, the spoons, knives, the salt shakers and cups, instead of putting them in the right place. Sometimes I watch how the extras are distributed or who sits next to whom. And I get some ideas. For if I do something, I never do it thoughtlessly. This waiter's job is of great use to me, it's pleasant and interesting.

But not this is important. It is something quite different. Something that I have spoken and written about many times, that I have been fighting against for the past thirty years, since the inception of the Children's Home, fighting without a hope of victory, without visible effect, but I don't want to and cannot abandon that fight.

My aim is that in the Children's Home there should be no soft work or crude work, no clever or stupid work, no clean or dirty work. No work for nice young ladies or for the mob. In the Children's Home, there should be no purely physical and no purely mental workers.

At the institution at Dzielna Street run by the City Council, they look at me with shock and disgust when I shake hands with the charwoman, even when she happens to be scrubbing the stairs and her hands are wet. But frequently I forget to shake hands with Dr. K., and I have not been responding to the bows of Drs. M. and B.

I respect honest workers. To me their hands are clean and I hold their opinions in high esteem.

The washerwoman and the janitor at Krochmalna Street used to be invited to join our meetings, not just to please them but in order to take their advice and benefit from their assistance as specialists in matters which would otherwise be left unresolved, i.e. be placed under paragraph 3.[5]

There was a joke in a weekly newspaper of twenty years ago. Actually not a joke but a witty comment.

Josek—I don't remember which one, there were many

5. Par. 3 of the Home's Code read: "The Court doesn't know how it was in fact, and thus refuses to consider the case."

of them—could not solve a problem in arithmetic. He tried hard and long, and finally said:

"I don't know how to do it. I place it under paragraph three."

No one is better or wiser because he is working in the storeroom rather than pushing the wheelbarrow. No one is better or wiser just because he can wield power. I am not better or wiser for signing the passes, or donation receipts. This brainless work could be done more conscientiously and better by a youngster from third or even second grade.

The collector of money, a rude woman, is a nobody to me. Mr. Lejzor is a fine fellow though he digs in the filth of the sewage pipes and canals. Miss Nacia would deserve respect from me if she peeled potatoes instead of being a typist. And it is not my fault that Miss Irka, the nurse, shifts the inferior jobs onto Mira and that Mrs. Roza Sztokman, whom I also respect, once in a while may not scrub the toilet or the kitchen floor just to have a rest.

In farming, this is called crop rotation. In hygiene and medicine—a change of climate. In church—an act of humility. The Pope is called Holy Father, big men kneel down before him and kiss his slipper. And, once a year, the Pope washes the feet of twelve beggars in the church.

The Jews are conceited and that is why they are despised. I believe this will change, perhaps soon. Meanwhile, please don't get cross with me for collecting the dishes or emptying the buckets in the toilet.

Whoever says, "physical work is dirty work," is lying. Worse still the hypocrite who says, "No one should be ashamed of any work," but picks for himself only clean work, avoids what is described as dirty work and thinks that he should keep out of the way of dirty work.

August 1, 1942

Whenever the stems of potato plants grew excessively, a heavy roller would be dragged over them to crush them so that the fruit in the ground could ripen better.

*

Did Marcus Aurelius read the wisdom of Solomon? How soothing is the effect of his memoirs.

*

I sometimes hate, or perhaps only try to oppose, certain individuals, such as H., or G., more than Germans; from their point of view they work, or rather plan, reasonably and efficiently. They are bound to be angry because people get in their way. Get in their way foolishly.

And I get in their way, too. They are even indulgent. They simply catch you and order you to stand in one place, not to walk about the streets, not to get in the way.

They do me a favor, since roaming about I might be hit by a stray bullet. And this way I am safe standing against the wall, and can calmly and carefully observe and think—spin the web of thoughts.

So I spin the web of thoughts.

*

A blind old Jew remained at the little town of Myszyniec. Leaning on a stick, he walked among the carts, the horses, the Cossacks and the artillery guns. What a cruel thing to leave a blind old man behind.[6]

6. Again recollection of World War I.

109

"They wanted to take him along"—Nastka says. "But he put his foot down and said that he would not go because somebody must stay behind to look after the synagogue."

I struck up an acquaintance with Nastka while trying to help her find a bucket taken by a soldier who had promised to bring it back but didn't.

I am both the blind Jew and Nastka.

*

It's so soft and warm in my bed. It'll be very hard to get up. But today is Saturday, and on Saturdays I weigh the children in the morning before breakfast. Probably for the first time I am not interested in the results for the week. They ought to have put on a bit of weight. (I don't know why raw carrot was given for supper yesterday.)

*

In place of old Azrylewicz, I now have young Julek. There's liquid in his side. He has certain difficulties with breathing, but for a different reason.

Here's the very same manner of groaning, gestures, resentment against me, the same selfish and theatrical desire to attract attention, perhaps even to take revenge on me for not thinking about him.

Today Julek had the first quiet night for a week. So did I.

*

So did I. Now that every day brings so many strange and sinister experiences and sensations I have completely ceased to dream.

110

The law of equilibrium.

The day torments, the night soothes. A gratifying day, a tormented night.

I could write a monograph on the featherbed.

The peasant and the featherbed.

The proletarian and the featherbed.

*

It's been a long time since I have blessed the world. I tried to tonight. It didn't work.

I don't even know what went wrong. The purifying respirations worked more or less. But the fingers remained feeble, no energy flowing through them.

Do I believe in the effects? I do believe but not in my India! Holy India!

*

The look of this district is changing from day to day.
1. A prison
2. A plague-stricken area
3. A mating ground
4. A lunatic asylum
5. A casino. Monaco. The stake—your head.

*

What matters is that all this did happen.

The destitute beggars suspended between prison and hospital. The slave work: not only the effort of the muscles but the honor and virtue of the girl.

Debased faith, family, motherhood.

The marketing of all spiritual commodities. A stock exchange quoting the weight of conscience. An unsteady market—like onions and life today.

111

The children are living in constant uncertainty, in fear. "A Jew will take you away." "I'll give you away to a wicked old man." "You'll be put in a bag."

Bereavement.

Old age. Its degradation and moral decrepitude.

(Once upon a time one earned one's old age, it was good to work for it. The same with health. Now the vital forces and the years of life may be purchased. A scoundrel has a good chance of achieving gray hair.)

*

Miss Esterka.

Miss Esterka is not anxious to live either gaily or easily. She wants to live nicely. She dreams of a beautiful life.

She gave us *The Post Office* as a farewell for the time being.[7]

If she does not come back here now, we shall meet later somewhere else. I'm absolutely sure that she will serve others in the meantime in the same way as she used to distribute goodness and make herself useful here.

7. This is about the tutoress Ester Winogron, a student of natural science at Warsaw University. She helped Korczak in his daily morning medical rounds and dressings. When she was caught by the Germans on the street in the first days of the liquidation of the ghetto, Korczak tried unsuccessfully to get her out of the transport.

As for the play itself, *The Post Office* by Rabindranath Tagore, prohibited by Hitler's censors, was performed on orders from Korczak himself. The direction of Ester Winogron and the performance of the children of the Orphan's Home, especially of Abrasza in the role of the dying Hindu boy, as well as the impact of the play itself, as played in the atmosphere of the dying ghetto, in the climate of its final days—all this produced a staggering impression and an experience not to be repeated.

When after the play someone asked Korczak why he had selected this particular play, he said that, finally, it is necessary to learn to accept serenely the angel of death.

112

August 4, 1942

1

I have watered the flowers, the poor orphanage plants, the plants of the Jewish orphanage. The parched soil breathed with relief.

A guard watched me as I worked. Does that peaceful work of mine at six o'clock in the morning annoy him or move him?

He stands looking on, his legs wide apart.

2

All the efforts to get Esterka released have come to nothing. I was not quite sure whether in the event of success I should be doing her a favor or harm her.

"Where did she get caught?" somebody asks.

Perhaps it is not she but we who have gotten caught (having stayed).

3

I have written to the police to send Adzio away: he's mentally underdeveloped and maliciously undisciplined. We cannot afford to expose the house to the danger of his outbursts. (Collective responsibility.)

4

For Dzielna Street—a ton of coal, for the present to Rozia Abramowicz. Someone asks whether the coal will be safe there.

In reply—a smile.

5

A cloudy morning. Five thirty.

Seemingly an ordinary beginning of a day. I say to Hanna:

"Good morning!"

In response, a look of surprise.
I plead:
"Smile."
They are ill, pale, lung-sick smiles.

6

You drank, and plenty, gentlemen officers, you re-
lished your drinking—here's to the blood you've shed—
and dancing you jingled your medals to cheer the infamy
which you were too blind to see, or rather pretended not
to see.

7

My share in the Japanese war. Defeat—disaster.
In the European war—defeat—disaster.
In the World War. . . .
I don't know how and what a soldier of a victorious
army feels. . . .

8

The publications to which I contributed were usually
closed down, suspended, went bankrupt.
My publisher, ruined, committed suicide.
And all this not because I'm a Jew but because I was
born in the East.
It might be a sad consolation that the haughty West
also is not well off.
It might be but is not. I never wish anyone ill. I cannot. I don't know how it's done.

9

Our Father who art in heaven. . . .
This prayer was carved out of hunger and misery.
Our daily bread.
Bread.

Why, what I'm experiencing did happen. It happened.

They sold their belongings—for a liter of lamp oil, a kilogram of groats, a glass of vodka.

When a young Pole kindly asked me at the police station how I managed to run the blockade, I asked him whether he could not possibly do "something" for Esterka.

"You know very well I can't."

I said hastily:

"Thanks for the kind word."

This expression of gratitude is the bloodless child of poverty and degradation.

10

I am watering the flowers. My bald head in the window. What a splendid target.

He has a rifle. Why is he standing and looking on calmly?

He has no orders to shoot.

And perhaps he was a village teacher in civilian life, or a notary, a street sweeper in Leipzig, a waiter in Cologne?

What would he do if I nodded to him? Waved my hand in a friendly gesture?

Perhaps he doesn't even know that things are—as they are?

He may have arrived only yesterday, from far away. . . .

Translated from the Polish
by JERZY BACHRACH
and BARBARA KRZYWICKA (VEDDER)

Korczak with members of his staff

*Postage stamps issued in Poland
and Israel commemorating Janusz Korczak*